Integrating Quality and Risk Management in Logistics

Authored by Marieta Stefanova

Published in London, United Kingdom

Integrating Quality and Risk Management in Logistics
http://dx.doi.org/10.5772/103050
Authored by Marieta Stefanova

Contributors
Marieta Stefanova

First published in London, United Kingdom, 2022 by IntechOpen
IntechOpen is the global imprint of INTECHOPEN LIMITED, registered in England and Wales, registration number: 11086078, 5 Princes Gate Court, London, SW7 2QJ, United Kingdom

British Library Cataloguing-in-Publication Data
A catalogue record for this book is available from the British Library

Additional hard and PDF copies can be obtained from orders@intechopen.com

Integrating Quality and Risk Management in Logistics
Authored by Marieta Stefanova
p. cm.
Print ISBN 978-1-80356-533-0
Online ISBN 978-1-80356-534-7
eBook (PDF) ISBN 978-1-80356-535-4

For EU product safety concerns:
IN TECH d.o.o., Prolaz Marije Krucifikse Kozulić 3, 51000 Rijeka, Croatia,
info@intechopen.com or visit our website at intechopen.com.

Meet the author

Marieta Stefanova, Ph.D., is an academic lecturer in the Department of Management and Logistics, Nikola Vaptsarov Naval Academy, Bulgaria. She teaches bachelor's-level courses in Logistics and Quality and master's-level courses in Quality Management, Safety, Environmental and Security Management, Logistics, Ship Agency, and Freight Forwarding. She has more than twenty-five years of professional experience as a quality manager in food manufacturing plants. Dr. Stefanova is a member of the Expert Council of the Center for Quality of Goods and Consumer Protection (CQGCP) at the Research Institute of the University of Economics (UE) – Varna. She is also a member of the Union of Scientists Bulgaria and the IGWT International Association for Commodity Science and Technology. She has published more than forty articles in national and international scientific journals.

Contents

Preface

This book focuses on the integration of quality and risk management in logistics. It examines theoretical and practical guidelines and addresses the main risks of non-compliance with the customer and legislative requirements that arise in a constantly changing external environment.

The research approach is to look for the synergistic effect of quality and risk management by applying appropriate tools for their integration based on the definition of the applicable conditional variables in the specific existing situation. The analyses conducted, give us a reason to believe that the development of a systematic approach, including both satisfaction analysis and risk factor analysis, may be sufficient grounds for initiating improvements in customer service.

Marieta Stefanova
Department of Management and Logistics,
Nikola Vaptsarov Naval Academy,
Varna, Bulgaria

Acknowledgements

First, I would like to thank my family for coping with my absence during the writing of this book, especially my husband Daniel Stefanov, without whose support I would not have been able to realise this idea.

A huge thank you to my colleagues at the Department of Management and Logistics for encouraging this project.

I also thank all the logistics companies and users of logistics services who participated in the survey and shared their experiences.

I thank all the scientific contributors who provided constructive criticism of my work and made valuable contributions to its completion.

I also thank the "N. Vaptsarov" Naval Academy for opening opportunities and providing access to world-class educational and scientific resources and assistance from distinguished professors with scientific interests in my research field.

Thank you to all the organisations that hired me as a consultant and helped me strive for lifelong learning.

Chapter 1

Changes in Quality and Risk Management in Logistics

Marieta Stefanova

'There is nothing so useless as doing with great efficiency something that should not be done at all.'

Peter Drucker

Abstract

For organizations providing logistics services, dynamic changes in the external environment impact process performance risk and threaten effective integration of resources, coordinated management of operations and consequently, negatively impact customer satisfaction and loyalty. These processes call for an improvement of logistics service management and an integrated management concept combining the integration of satisfaction analysis processes and the risks that can negatively impact the delivery of a satisfying logistics service. The study focuses on the integration of quality and risk management in the supply chain to examine the theoretical and practical guidelines and address the main risks of non-compliance with the customer and legislative requirements that arise in a constantly changing external environment. The research approach is to look for the synergistic effect of quality and risk management by applying appropriate tools for their integration based on the definition of the applicable conditional variables in the specific existing situation. The analysis conducted to give us reason to believe that the development of a systematic approach, including both satisfaction analysis and risk factor analysis, may be sufficient grounds for initiating improvements in customer service.

Keywords: quality, risk management, logistics

1. Introduction

Drucker's postulate that the most serious mistakes are made not because of wrong answers but of wrong questions provoked the writing of this monograph. Every day, we are inundated with information about various leaders worldwide who have taken charge and solved yet another global problem in the right way. Solving any problem, unfortunately, can only restore the equilibrium that existed before the problem occurred. There is a lack of information on how crises arising from dynamic changes and emerging risks in the external environment can create favorable conditions for other leaders who see these as an opportunity to seek the path of innovation, develop their potential and transform into a more favorable outcome.

The positive effects of quality management have long been established in the scientific literature. If we compile a basic list of these effects, it would undoubtedly include cost reductions, better relationships with suppliers and customers, just-in-time deliveries, reduced waste, increased added value for customers, and better conditions for developing market potential. These benefits can also be applied to quality management in logistics.

Logistics is a key activity for any business idea. The challenges of market change require continuous improvement of supply chain performance and, in this process, quality improvement through risk analysis is important. Risk is always associated with uncertainty, therefore, to reach a new improved level of logistics services, processes must be managed and analyzed with appropriate methods. Quality management is based on conditional variables that are determined by the changing market conditions in a specific time span. Modern logistics firms are increasingly focused on improving supply chain performance, where improvement with quality management is the primary mechanism for achievement. This study seeks to identify the ways to achieve better business process performance in logistics services through the application of basic quality and risk management tools. There is no single correct approach or the best tool for quality management in logistics. It is necessary to find an approach that incorporates contingencies and the current market situation and to analyze and identify an effective service improvement strategy applicable to the changing circumstances. The research approach is to look for the synergistic effect of quality and risk management by applying appropriate tools for their integration based on the definition of the applicable conditional variables in the specific existing situation.

2. Factors influencing the imposition of changes in the attributes for assessing the quality of logistics services

In late 2019, a new type of viral disease called coronavirus (COVID-19) was discovered in the provincial capital of Hubei [1–3] and within a few months, its spread spanned the globe. Many researchers support the view that urbanization and increasing population density are major catalysts for the spread of COVID-19 [3–5]. The outbreak of the COVID-19 pandemic has forced authorities worldwide to introduce restrictions and bans on the movement of people and goods throughout the supply chain. In response to these challenges, most countries have announced national travel and transport bans to certain regions [6]. The introduction of restrictions has become a huge challenge for all logistics stakeholders [2, 7], which include producers, municipal authorities, inspection bodies, medical practitioners, household purchasing decision-makers, managers deciding on the organization of order fulfillment in the supply chain, and many others [8–10]. The constraints and longer vehicle dwell times at border controls and entry and exit points in the country of delivery have necessitated an increase in shipping costs and prevented the necessary quantities of essential goods from being secured and stock reserves replenished. One of the conditions for quality management in logistics—those goods arrive on time—became an unenforceable condition for deliveries from locations where COVID-19 restrictions were imposed.

Quality management decisions in logistics activities during this period were driven by the importance of the role of logistics in supply management and the constraints introduced by government authorities. During a pandemic, stockpiling essentials and personal protective equipment for the population is a difficult challenge for the entire logistics chain [2, 11–14]. The threat of the rapid spread of disease requires logistics organizations to respond quickly to ensure the seamless supply of personal protective equipment, disinfectants, medicines, medical supplies, essential foods, among others [2–4, 15, 16].

The constraints create risk-laden conditions managing the quality of logistics processes and making effective decisions related to capacity, choice, and use of means of transport, and compromise the performance of the supply chain processes [17–21].

The high population density in large population centers and living close to large retail chains have limited the ability to supply less accessible and remote areas with the same resources. A cost-effective method of redistribution through logistics was not implemented in the short term. The effort to limit the spread of the virus has created unaffordable conditions for the implementation of basic logistics activities and services. Household decision-makers reacted quickly to the changed conditions and stocked personal protective equipment and invested in commodities that had a limited shelf life, which required them to be discarded at a later stage. Fear of the shortage of goods anticipated due to the restrictions on the movement of vehicles created panic in the population [22–24] and, consequently, a glut of goods. This process triggered a new wave of shortages throughout the supply chain caused by the irregularity of consumption compared to the previous period and the depletion of goods due to overstocking [16, 25]. Households did not make purchase decisions based on their actual and expected consumption for future time periods.

The pandemic has forced households to increase their online purchases and reduce their visits to retail outlets [26–28], even for necessities and everyday purchases. Traditional order fulfillment approaches proved inadequate for the changed market conditions as consumers demanded that logistics service providers fulfill their orders within the day or within a few hours [29]. Some retail logistics chains have proved unprepared to provide their customers with full online real-time delivery traceability and prioritize task fulfillment by optimizing the solution of the same tasks on the fly. The introduction of various supply chain applications has allowed the most proactive in the industry to perform full supply chain traceability and help share information quickly with customers when deliveries are delayed.

The surge in essential goods has hampered all logistics operations in delivering on time [30–32] and resulted in an inability to meet planned and agreed quantities between the business partners managing them.

The COVID-19 pandemic forced rapid changes in logistics development and catalyzed the creation of new business models for query management. The path to adapt to the new normal requires the introduction of more automated processes and technologies to facilitate the processing of requests coming in via e-commerce [33]. There is a requirement to introduce a new, rethought supply chain business approach based on trust, value-added processes, and tolerance when contractual terms cannot be met because of restrictions. To achieve compliant logistics service performance is increasingly impossible without coordination between all stakeholders and real-time decision-making. Dynamic changes in the environment have become a major factor for quality process performance requiring a high degree of synchronization and collaboration [34–37].

These developments have positively impacted inventory turnover but caused a boom in order fulfillment wherein quality control processes for performance management have been limited and, in some cases, even neglected. Reduced process controls have worsened the performance quality of set execution procedures. Quality management in logistics is concerned with delivering products on time, in the required quantity, and at the location specified by the customer. Due to the irregularity of deliveries resulting from the above reasons, warehouse space proved insufficient to cover the restocking of goods for increased consumption. The inadequacy of the existing infrastructure to conduct logistics operations, warehousing bottlenecks, and the breakdown of agreements between stakeholders on the supply and distribution of essential food and medical supplies are among the most debated topics in the literature [38, 39].

The increased frequency of emergency deliveries has necessitated the commitment of additional resources for the implementation of logistics processes, which are not always available during crisis situations and, therefore, has hampered the efficiency of processes and deteriorated the quality of their implementation. Accordingly, planned audits of the logistics quality management systems were not carried out and, in many cases, these were not carried out in their entirety and according to the planned measures. This created the conditions for impaired decision-making that ignored one of the basic data-driven principles of logistics quality management and caused confusion and delays in meeting agreed and contracted delivery quantities. Overstocking of products has also deteriorated the quality of value-added services, such as additional picking, repacking, and labeling. Overstocking of warehouse space has significantly impaired the implementation of replenishment policies as stock capacity is limited. The overloading of warehouse staff has delayed the decision-making about time schedules and workforce allocation.

Maintaining the quality of logistics services during a pandemic requires making the right and meaningful efforts to address the challenges posed by a dynamic changing environment. The application of a multidisciplinary approach and the coordination between all stakeholders actively involved in logistics processes have the potential to limit quality deterioration and other inconsistencies and are, perhaps, the only prerequisite for the success of these activities. Lack of coordination creates uncertainty in the fulfillment of customer requirements and implementation of planned quality management activities in logistics.

The risk of quality deterioration in logistics services increases manifold due to inefficient communication with customers in the event of delivery-related difficulties and reverse logistics of goods returned due to delays. Quality management in logistics has the potential to help ensure the proper distribution of essential goods during the period of retrenchment.

Some factors affecting supply chain management operations during a pandemic [40–42], have been the subject of many scientific publications and have been studied by several authors [43]. Quality assurance in logistics processes creates the prerequisites of a positive image for logistics brands to achieve a lasting trend of customer loyalty and competitive advantage [44, 45]. During the COVID-19 crisis, quality assurance was mainly related to the safety of supply and the reliability of supply chains.

Therefore, to build the resilience of logistics processes in the face of dynamic environmental changes and emerging supply security risks and threats, organizations need to more clearly and accurately analyze the factors that help establish and ensure logistics service quality and customer satisfaction.

The study identifies the key factors that help to make the right logistics decisions for quality management in times of risk and dynamic changes in the environment. During a crisis from the external environment, the results show that quality management is introduced after the fact and is mainly related to corrective rather than preventive actions. This calls for a more in-depth investigation and concrete solutions for quality management through risk management in logistics, which is the main objective of the analyses in the different chapters of this study.

Replace the entirety of this text with the introduction to your chapter. The introduction section should provide a context for your manuscript and should be numbered as the first heading. When preparing the introduction, please bear in mind that some readers will not be experts in your field of research.

3. Current aspects of quality management in logistics

Considering the rapid changes in market conditions worldwide and as a result of the measures taken to physically distance and restrict access to ports due to the COVID-19 pandemic, there is no active physical communication between the user and the logistics service provider. Well-known quality assessment methods in most cases provide for such a communication and survey of user expectations. Some of the variables studied in these methods assess the logistics environment and evaluate the customers' direct communication at the physical level of the employees performing the services (e.g. uniform and appearance).

This chapter presents some of the main and most popular methods, their key parameters, advantages, and disadvantages in their application for discussion. The most applicable models that have the potential to be used for quality assessment, in particular for the assessment of logistics services, are studied.

The study of the different service quality management models aims to assess their suitability and adequacy or need for improvement. Different standards and good practices for quality management have been practically identified, which, of course, also have different objectives. This makes their application difficult because often no clear distinction is made between a specification (which sets out requirements) and codes of good practice (recommending a course of action) in their use.

Customers have been found to rate the quality of service whether it is good or poor [46–51]. Scholars opine that service quality is determined by the differences between expectations and perception of the service received [52–54]. It is undisputed that service quality is essential. What happens when the quality of logistics services is higher than expected and how to prevent the negative impact of various risk factors that could compromise high quality? Some researchers believe that customer satisfaction with the quality of certain services will determine the failure or success of a company [44, 55–64]. The main problem with measuring the quality of any service is related to its inherent characteristics: intangibility [65, 66], heterogeneity, and indivisibility. Accordingly, quality cannot be measured before the service is provided to the customer, unlike goods whose quality can be measured at any time [67]. Researchers agree that measuring the level of service quality is difficult but they have conflicting views on how logistics organizations overcome this difficulty in practice, regardless of what assessment methodology is used. Some researchers have segmented the market based on different types of logistics services [68, 69], some have studied the level of logistics services by different economic sectors [70], and others have studied the level of quality by geographical market segmentation, such as Vietnam [48], India [71], and Serbia [72].

Quality management activities are related to compliance with many standardization documents—various technical specifications, manuals, process management codes, and guidelines by various international organizations [73]. An important difference between standards and other documents is the level of consensus required for their approval. Standards and technical specifications contain requirements to which processes or services must conform (normative requirements), whereas other types of documents contain only recommendations. The main problem associated with quality assessment in the service area is the contradiction between the customers' and service providers' perceptions of quality service. Customers want to receive services of the highest quality according to their perceptions of excellent quality and service providers are looking for solutions that match their requirements and expectations.

Logistics firms have long viewed logistics not just as an area for cost improvement, but as a key source of competitive advantage within the firm's overall marketing efforts. The quality performance of all these processes requires the integration of different activities and compliance control for pre-set criteria.

Researchers note that there are some basic and critically important indicators for the perception of consistent logistics service quality: timeliness [69, 74–77], availability [78], and order compliance.

4. Quality assessment indicators

Although many researchers support the view that logistics services complement the marketing efforts of sales organizations, there is a lack of well-founded evidence on the meaning of logistics service quality and its essential attributes for customer evaluation. Little research has been done to identify the differences in quality assessment attributes for different market segments and, consequently, how these attributes change under the impact of risks from the external environment. There is also insufficient research on the impact of dynamic environmental changes on quality management models and concepts in logistics in particular. The different attributes for assessing the quality of logistics services differ for each market segment and they are radically different for services that customers request over the Internet and through direct contact. This suggests that firms need to adapt their logistics services to changes in the external environment and customer orientation primarily toward Internet commerce during the pandemic.

Adding unobservable attributes that are essential to customers' perceived value of logistics services to the traditionally measured set of operational attributes to evaluate services.

Quality management involves the management of processes in a unified system. Logistics processes require efforts to be focused on the delivery of material flows by managing the selection and supplier performance improvement to just-in-time delivery of goods and customer service.

When measuring and analyzing quality in logistics, the first step is to determine the appropriate attributes for their corresponding level. Delivery time is the most used metric. There is no need for evidence confirming delivery delays as the most frequent cause of deterioration in the expected level of quality and customer dissatisfaction. Timeliness of delivery is cited by many researchers as the most important indicator for measuring quality [79–84]. Among the most important quality indicators in logistics, the following have been mentioned by various sources: the quantity of orders fulfilled (matching the requested items), the quantity of orders processed per unit time, timely and complete product delivery information given to customers, personal contact with staff, the accuracy of fulfilled orders, the status of products received in orders, and prompt and timely response to order discrepancies. The impact of the logistics firm's corporate image, the ability to handle non-standard logistics services, and the ability to technically execute the service are examined as additional indicators to assess quality.

These metrics have priorities differing by industry, such as when logistics is part of the functional departments of manufacturing companies the metrics are related to on-time delivery, error-free delivery, and lead time. In transport logistics, the quality assessment attributes are mainly: reliability of delivery, assurance of performance, payment options, and transfer of insurance and other risks. An interesting indicator that has become increasingly important in recent years is the possibility of reverse logistics and buyback.

Logistics service quality indicators are associated with several possible attributes:

- Reliability of logistics [85–88]
- Value provided to the client [72, 89–91]
- Logistical flexibility [85, 86, 92–94]
- Quality of logistics services [8, 34, 35, 95, 96]
- Indicators related to export and import procedures. Nordås and Grosso have an interesting study on the impact of lengthy export and import procedures on logistics processes and the creation of strict trade barriers [97]
- Logistical errors in delivery [30, 98–101]
- Indicators related to lead time:
- Timeliness of delivery [101, 102]
- Query execution time [103, 104]
- Just-in-time delivery [105–107]
- Processing time for orders and requests [108]
- Logistical lead time [78, 109, 110]
- Process performance indicators:
- Quality of feedback and personal contact with employees in the logistics company [80, 111]
- Conditions in the customer request related to minimum quantity or promotional offer [78]

- Accuracy of the prepared request in accordance with the customer's preferences [112]
- The use, acceptance, and exchange of information with customers [78, 113–115]
- The procedures for the preparation of requests [116]
- Increase the number of requests sent by customers [117, 118]

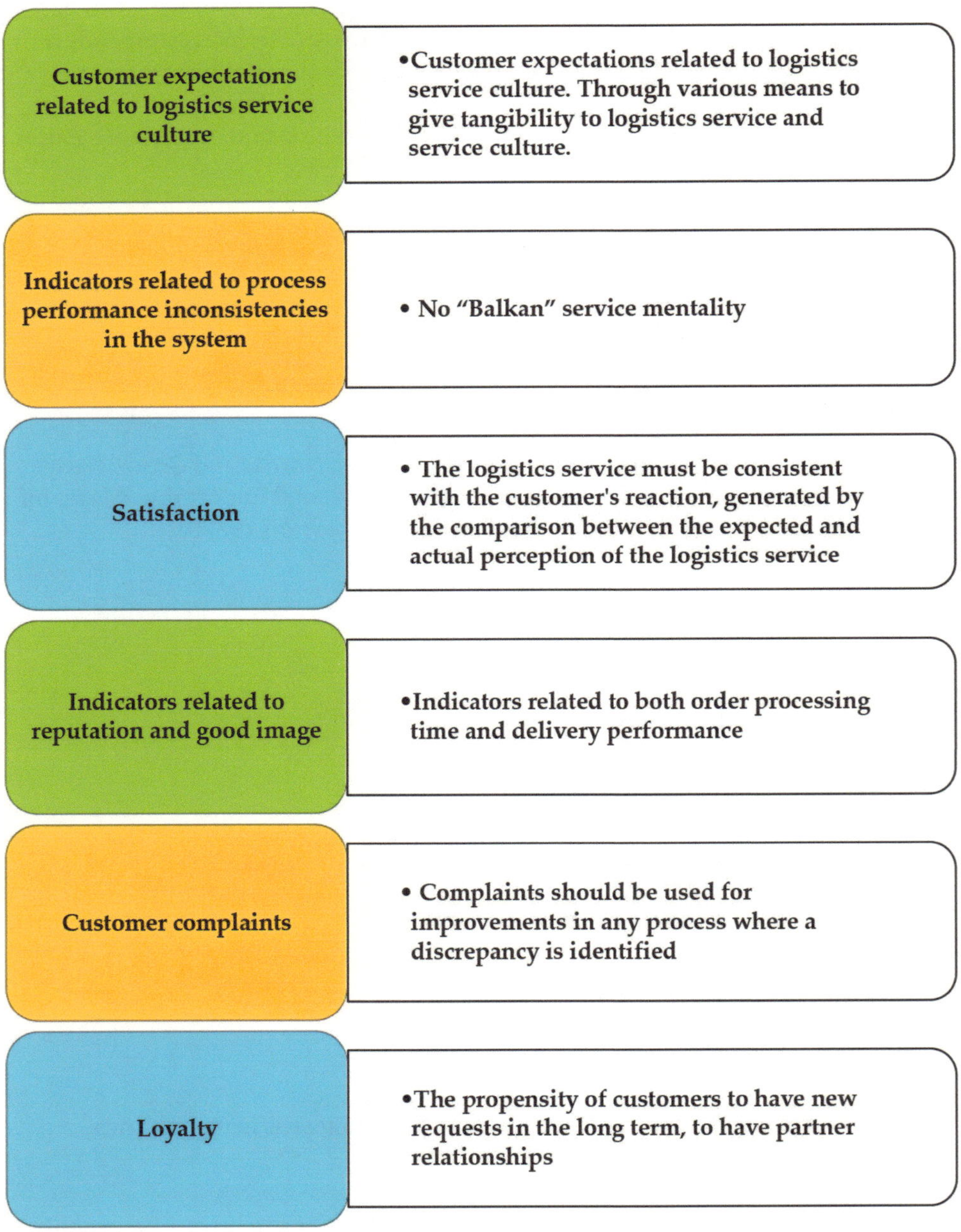

Figure 1.
Key indicators for measuring logistics service quality.

- Quality of requests related to promotional items and value of the total requested quantity [74, 119]

- Speed and authority in handling discrepancies in the preparation of requests [111]

- Customer satisfaction [54, 67, 120–123]. Customer satisfaction depends on many factors related to the perceived quality of services provided, the emotional state of customers, social interaction, customer experience, and other specific subjective factors. Several researchers support the view that customer satisfaction with service quality is not an objective assessment of the actual situation but an emotional factor. Customer satisfaction is primarily associated with the evaluation of process outcomes and can be viewed as a positive evaluation of the service by the customer (**Figure 1**).

5. Service quality assessment models and methods

The literature describes many quality assessment methods that can be used to help service providers understand whether they are partially or fully meeting client requirements. The differences in methods are based on different criteria for assessing the mismatch between clients' expectations of the service and their perception of the service consumed. It is generalizable about all methods that to conduct them, information from the customers' service evaluation needs to be analyzed, which means that customers are actively involved in the process. How can prospective customers who have not yet received the service evaluate it? These surveys, therefore, involve customers who have already received services. The whole market is relevant for the logistics organization, specifically, why did the other customers in logistics choose the competitor's company? Another question that arises is how the opinion of those who do not use logistics companies but build their own logistics departments within production sites can be investigated.

5.1 Grönroos (1984) technical and functional quality model

The Grönroos model surveys a sample of business managers who are users of an existing and used service to test its perceived quality [46, 124]. Grönroos' study supports the view that quality indicators are interrelated and there is a causal relationship between them. Quality assessment under this model compares the customer's expected and perceived quality of service to measure user satisfaction. Grönroos identifies three components of service quality, namely: technical quality; functional quality; and image quality [124] (**Figure 2**).

The main criticism of Grönroos model is that this model does not assign different weighting factors to the overall evaluation of the service delivered, but only emphasizes the importance of functional quality. This critical flaw prevents the result of the measurement by the model to be an objective evaluation with practical application, but only stating the factors are interrelated. Several researchers have studied the method [125] and others have explored its practical application [126, 127]. Some researchers have criticized the method, empirically proving that there is no causal relationship between technical quality, image, and perceived quality and the relationships between these three aspects of quality are not significant [128]. To date, the paper describing the method has been cited 12,219 times in other scientific publications according to the Google Science website.

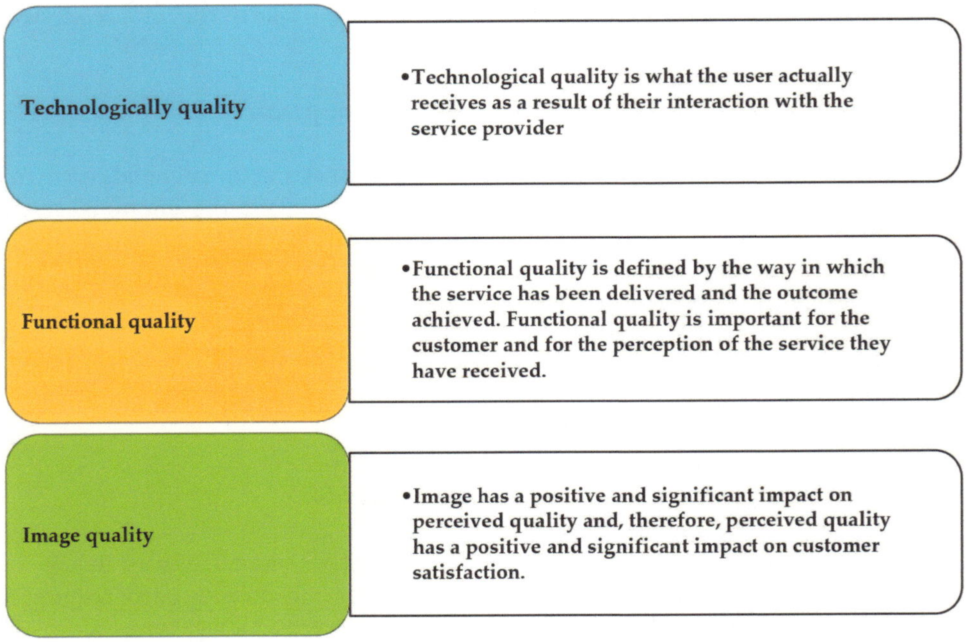

Figure 2.
Components of the Grönroos model (adapted [124]).

5.2 The European customer satisfaction index model

The European Customer Satisfaction Index (EPSI) model, first introduced in 1999 as a method for modeling and predicting customer satisfaction, has been extensively studied by many researchers in the field of quality management [129–134]. This method is based on the seven indices of the EPSI summary index. Sweden was the first country to introduce the index as the main method to measure customer satisfaction in different industries (SCSB). In 1994, the method was adapted to the American Customer Satisfaction Index (ACSI) [134, 135]. A few years later, after several publications and recommendations from the EOQ (European Organization for Quality) and EFQM (European Foundation for Quality Management), the EPSI was established as the main tool for measuring customer satisfaction in Europe [136–138]. When customer satisfaction is measured through surveys, several key issues arise, the main one being the collection and aggregation of survey data.

This issue is defined more clearly and determined by the structure and content of the satisfaction survey questionnaire and the method by which the sample size will be determined.

5.3 Logistics Performance Index

The Logistics Performance Index (LPI) is an indicator that measures the performance of retail supply chains or logistics performance and is produced by the World Bank every 2 years. Comparative data on the composite indicators of the index for the last 5 years are presented in **Figure 3**. The data defining the index was collected through a survey of international academic institutions, organizations, and individuals active in the global logistics market. Respondents assign scores by rating the result

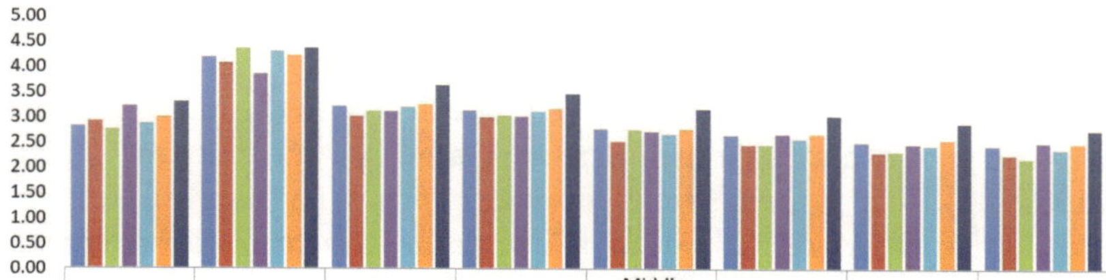

	Bulgaria	Germany	Europe & Central Asia	East Asia & Pacific	Middle East & North Africa	Latin America & Caribbean	South Asia	Sub-Saharan Africa
LPI Score	2.841196	4.2	3.24	3.15	2.78	2.66	2.51	2.45
Customs	2.937588	4.09	3.04	3.01	2.54	2.47	2.32	2.27
Infrastructure	2.762986	4.37	3.13	3.05	2.76	2.47	2.33	2.2
International shipments	3.233723	3.86	3.14	3.03	2.73	2.69	2.48	2.52
Logistics competence	2.881315	4.31	3.21	3.13	2.68	2.59	2.45	2.39
Tracking & tracing	3.015289	4.24	3.27	3.18	2.79	2.68	2.56	2.5
Timeliness	3.313491	4.39	3.65	3.49	3.19	3.05	2.9	2.77

Figure 3.
Logistics performance index. Source: Compiled from World Bank data (database: LPI), last updated: 10/29/2019, available at: https://databank.banquemondiale.org).

on a scale from 1 (worst) to 5 (best). Each of the indicators measured relates to an assessment of the overall level of skills and quality of logistics services and the scores are averaged across all respondents.

Trade and transport have been found to stimulate economic development and improve national competitiveness. The index allows these developments to be compared against the same reliable logistical criteria. The World Bank's Logistics Performance Index (LPI) is this unique comparative tool. For example, the aggregated Logistics Efficiency Index (2018) ranks Bulgaria 52 out of 160 countries with an average score of 3.03. Some of the examined parameters by year, assessed on a 5-point rating scale, are presented in **Figure 3**.

The competence indicator of those engaged in logistics services at the national level throughout the reporting period has little variation in the scores awarded by the experts. The report, published after the survey, examined the direct correlation between deteriorating service quality indicators as a trade barrier and foreign direct investment in the sector [139].

The assessment of the logistics quality level must, of course, be evaluated by each market segment and, as a prerequisite, customer satisfaction must be surveyed. Negative assessments of quality are, in most cases, caused by risks that have not been sufficiently managed, for which a root cause analysis is necessary. Opportunities exist to assess user satisfaction and take prompt corrective action in cases with understated ratings. Quality is defined as "the degree to which a set of intrinsic characteristics of an object satisfy requirements" and a necessary condition for measuring quality is to define these requirements.

The requirements for logistics services originate from not only customers but also legislation applicable to the activity, stakeholders, and many others. The task is to ensure compliance with quality requirements and eliminate or minimize the impact of risks from logistics services or processes.

The need to integrate a multitude of activities requires quality management to focus on rapid change and flexibility in addressing the risks for the logistics organization to adapt to rapidly changing external circumstances.

5.4 The SERVQUAL model

In the last decade, the SERVQUAL model has been the most popular method for assessing service quality, which was first stated by Parasuraman, Zeithaml, and Berry in 1985 [67]. One of their articles, of only 14 pages, has nearly 6000 references to date [120] and the original article of 9 pages has nearly 37,000 references [67], while the improved methodology 3 years later has 40,000 [121].

The SERVQUAL model is a framework for service management [140] incorporating the core tasks of quality management with a focus on service quality. The main purpose of the SERVQUAL model is the comparison between perceptions and expectations that determine quality assessment and customer satisfaction.

The issue at hand is to measure customer expectations of logistics services given that the manifestation of these expectations is directly dependent on how customers interpret the environmental factors influencing the formation of expectations. The problems are exacerbated by the fact that some influencing factors may be within the control of the logistics firm, and therefore predictable, but other factors, such as psychological factors, are directly dependent on the customers themselves. Thus, logistics companies are challenged to ensure a clearer picture of their customers' expectations, which can be the basis to chart a concrete path toward meeting it more fully. The SERVQUAL model may be applied to achieve this goal, which refers to the following three main postulates (**Figure 4**).

The main analyses to be performed by logistics firms when applying the model are shown in **Figure 5**.

The model used to conduct the main analyses and which can be used by logistics companies are shown in **Figure 6**.

5.5 Contemporary aspects of service quality measurement in logistics

There are many different views on quality management in logistics. Perceptions of consistent quality in logistics services are quite different from the perspective of the activity manager and customer. Too often the quality criteria of the customer are quite different from those of those providing the logistics service. These reasons necessitate an exploration of different perspectives and appropriate means and methods to resolve the differences in these perceptions. Defining service quality is even more difficult than product quality. The main criteria for service quality are reliability and individual treatment by the organization providing them. To achieve compliance with

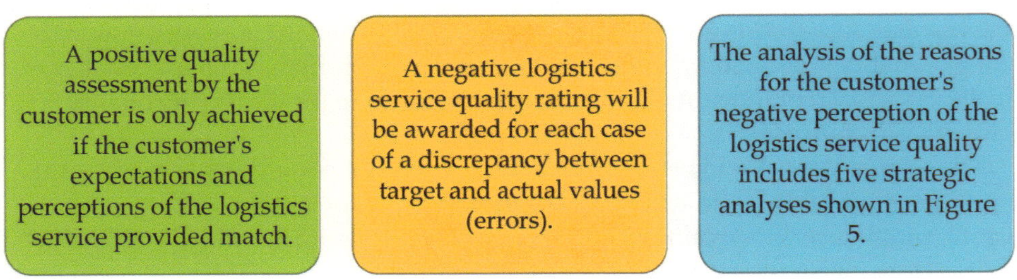

Figure 4.
Main postulates of the SERVQUAL model source: [121].

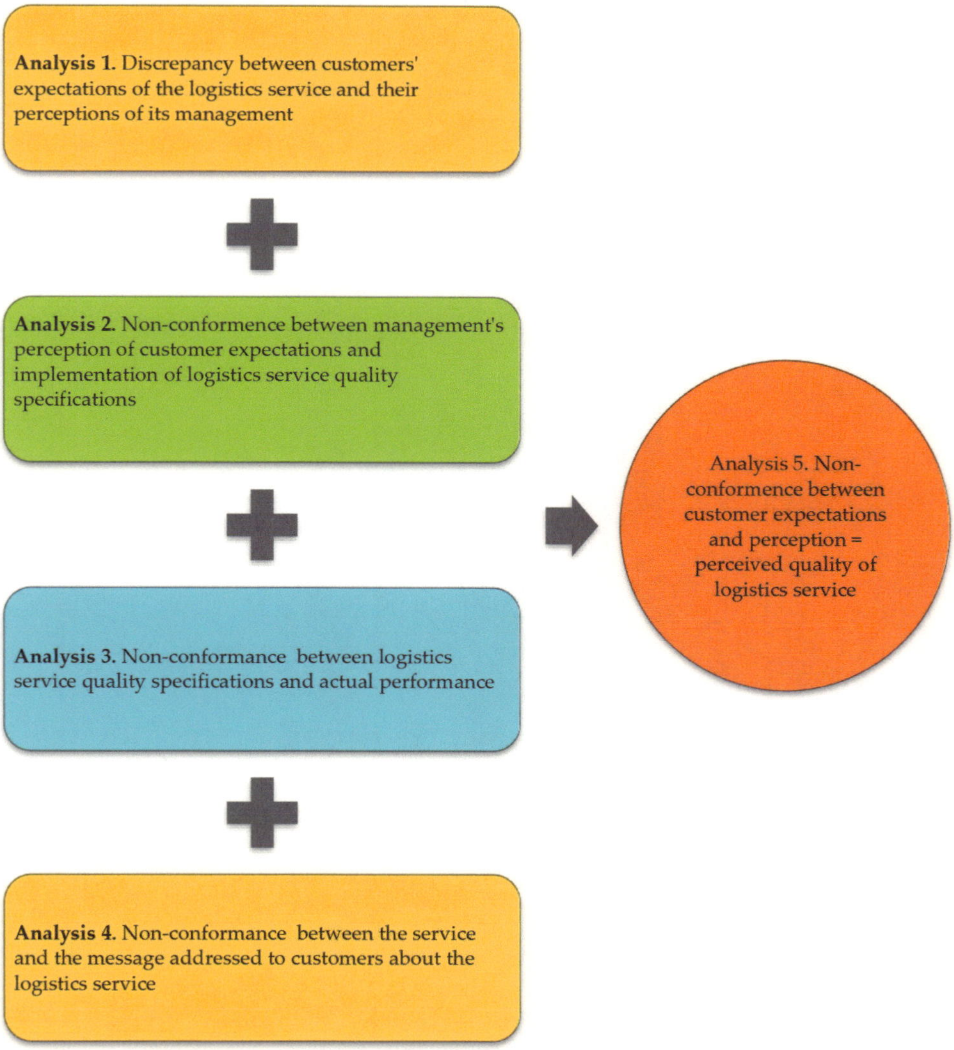

Figure 5.
CAP analyses of the SERVQUAL model in logistics services source: Adapted [121].

these indicators, all employees must be involved in its management to conduct the activity, which meets the customer's expectations. Unfortunately, there are fundamental differences between the ways that different departments of an organization perceive quality. The main reason for the emergence of non-conforming logistics processes is precisely this difference in perceptions of conforming quality as well as underestimation of its importance to the prosperity of the company.

The ways to solve these problems are related to effective communication and smoothing the differences between the different functional areas to achieve a service that meets the customer's needs. The task becomes more complex when you add the impact of external and internal environmental changes on the matching quality criteria for a particular supply, service, or process by regulators and stakeholders.

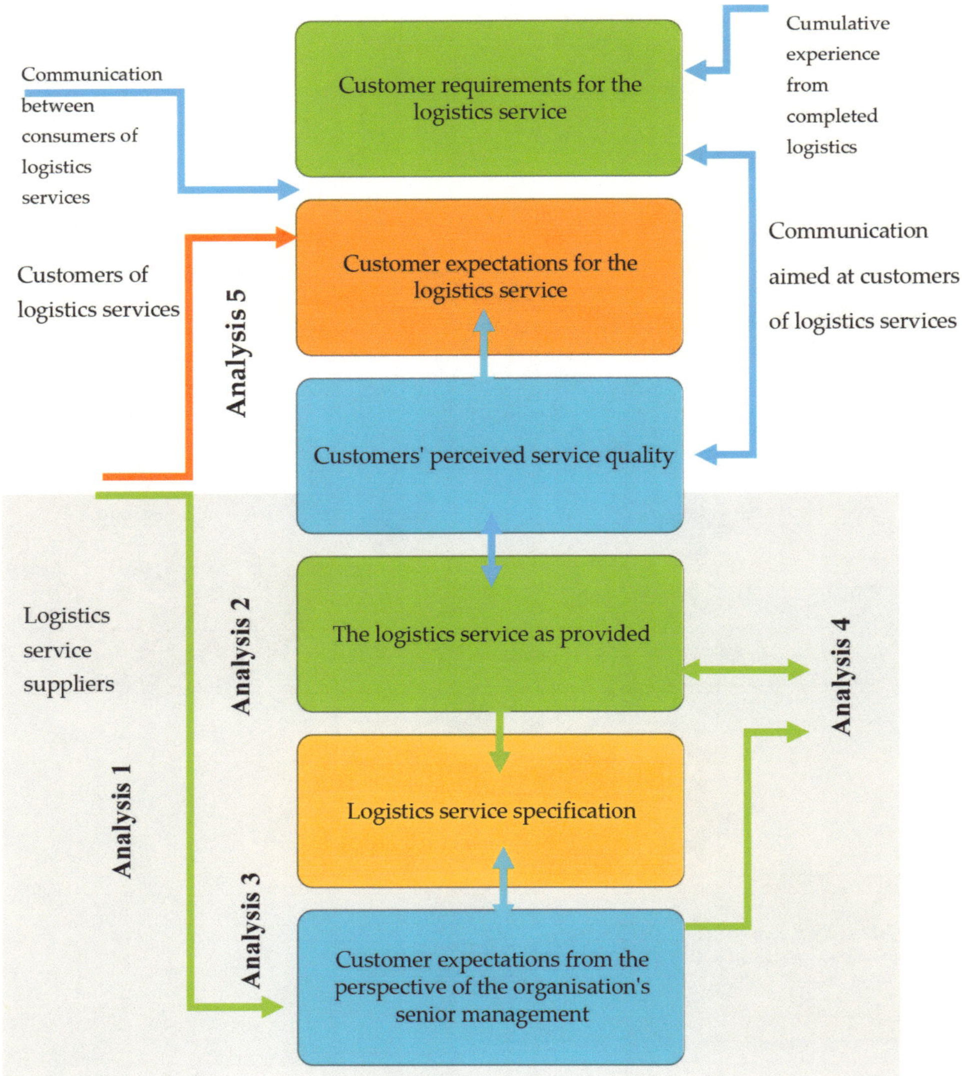

Figure 6.
SERVQUAL model processes in logistics services. Source: Adapted from Parasuraman, Zeithaml, Berry [121].

6. Risk management in logistics

Risk management in logistics and supply chains has been studied by many researchers. Their results confirm that mitigation opportunities depend on multiple interrelated factors and each of them can be the cause of drastic risk reduction if used wisely.

Most studies agree that adequate planning for the diversity of service offerings is the critical causal factor and can unlock a series of risk mitigation responses throughout the supply chain [141–144]. The next most important cause is the flexibility of supply contracts [142, 145–148].

These major risks can be managed if, based on the cause-effect relationships between different factors, work is done to reduce the overall impact of the risk.

Risk management actions make it possible for the support function of logistics services to remain in the background and become a crucial factor for the market success of the business operation. According to Fuchs and Wohinz [149], it is also necessary to clarify that research does not often clearly distinguish between the concepts of supply chain-wide risks and logistics risks.

Risks are described as unplanned events in the scientific literature, which does not imply a lack of preparation to manage them. For supply chains, logistics risks are related to the main service objectives: the lack of appropriate and customer-required goods, in the required delivery time, in the specified location, in the required quality.

Quality management activities and their associated risks identify the likelihood of risks before they occur and may, accordingly, affect the conditional allocation of losses in advance. The costs of remediation can be summarized in three main groups:

- Financial costs: once the non-conformity has been identified and action is taken to rectify it, the logistics organization must cover any damages to the customer. Studies find that the cost of correcting non-conformities is greater than what could have been spent on prevention in the planning process. The costs of recalling products and covering all reverse logistics activities are often excluded from the selling price of logistics services and are covered by the contingency and extraordinary costs line item.

- Survival costs: in most cases, inconsistencies in processes entail, at least, legal consequences. Larger inconsistencies can be a challenge to business survival as restitution damages can drag a logistics organization into insolvency.

- Reputation costs: inconsistencies in logistics operations and processes will, in most cases, result in customer backlash and a reduction in profit to cover losses from a reduction in planned sales.

Risk minimization and opportunity identification activities can be carried out in four phases:

- Plan risk management actions by setting the risk management framework.

- Implement actions to address risks in each logistics process.

- Monitor and analyze performance management actions to minimize risks and uncover opportunities by monitoring and analyzing the strategic risk management framework.

- Continuous improvement.

Logistics risks are generally associated with disruption of the planned material flow for any period [150–152]. Unexpected events or the reasons for their occurrence affect and hinder the supply of material flows of goods at an acceptable price.

Risk management in logistics is needed as an alternative to commercial insurance in cases where insurance coverage is limited or very costly. Preventive measures to manage risks are a form of insurance applied to assumed but unspecified events for which the probabilities and financial consequences are unknown. Various authors have studied the classification of the causes of supply chain risks in particular logistics, such as Essaber and Fuchs, whose work is one of the most generalized [149, 153, 154]. Based on these studies, four main causes of risk in logistics are outlined as shown in **Figure 7**.

Operational risks are caused in the normal course of logistics operations and are often related to disruptions in the supply chain of the goods to be transported and stored [155–159]. This risk creates insurmountable conditions that make the delivery of the goods in the volume and assortment desired by the customer impossible.

Operational risks can be caused by the malfunction or insufficiency of warehouse equipment and transport vehicles and also by external factors, such as incorrect choice of transport of the supplier of goods, excessive complexity in transport routes, failure of transport infrastructure, incorrect choice of transport packaging of supplies, failures, malfunctions, and accidents during the delivery of cargo [155–158].

Financial risks have been studied in many aspects along with different ways to overcome them by researchers who consider several main causes, such as poor cash

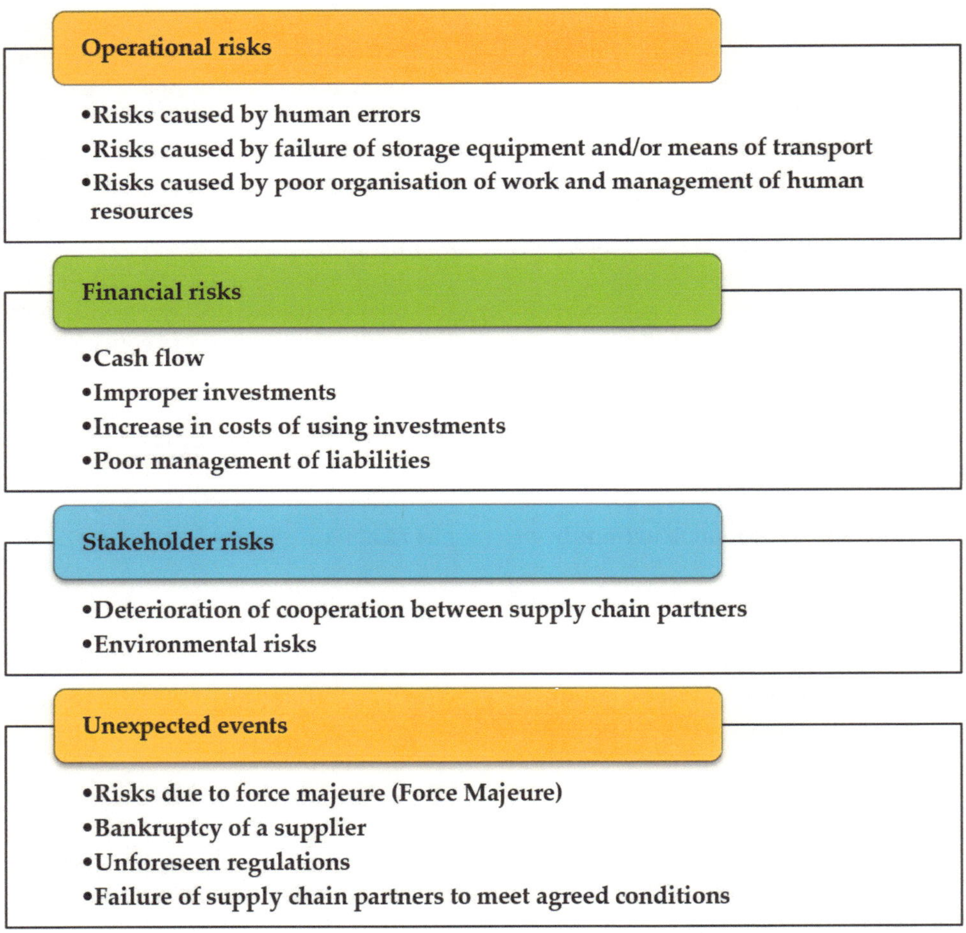

Figure 7.
Causes of risks in logistics services.

flow management, investments in inappropriate time periods under restrictive conditions, inflating costs for the use of investments, and falling out of interest rates that do not meet market conditions, poor management of liabilities [159]. Financial risks adversely affect the firm's overall operations and financial stability. These risks are often related to inadequate management of cash flows between organizations, excessive investments to enter new market segments, mismanagement or lack of coordination between the repayment of liabilities and expected receivables, the movement of cash between subsidiaries and related companies, sudden changes in tariff rates and tax legislation in the country of the raw material supplier.

Stakeholder-related risks stem from a deteriorating collaboration between supply chain partners. Environmental risks in logistics have the potential to negatively impact the environment [160, 161]. Stakeholder risks arise from supply chain disruption resulting from unanticipated rapid changes in the political environment and regulations, such as changes in tax rates, bans imposed by decree, embargoes, government bans and seizures, litigation, hacking, theft, and many others [162–165].

Risks associated with unexpected events arise primarily from risks posed by force majeure (e.g. natural disasters; international terrorist actions; economic crises; and port, terminal, and land border closures and strikes). The severity of the risk is calculated by the outcome of the adverse event, which often affects the financial stability of the company and its ability to deliver services, the timeliness of delivery of goods, and impairs the quality of performance of commitments made [166]. Another type of risk is the increasing degree of cooperation between supply chain partners which can make it difficult to take quick and adequate decisions due to the different interests and priorities of the partners involved. Risks that lead to a breakdown in performance can also be caused by the bankruptcy of a supplier, deterioration of quality control by the supplier, a series of planning errors, and overly complex automated decision-making systems for delivery routes. Another risk that is difficult to predict relates to the failure of supply chain partners to meet their commitments and/or agreed terms.

7. Conclusions

Although many researchers support the view that logistics services complement the marketing efforts of sales organizations, there is a lack of well-founded evidence on the meaning of logistics service quality and its essential attributes for customer evaluation. Adding unobservable attributes that are essential to customers' perceived value of logistics services to the traditionally measured set of operational attributes to evaluate services. Quality management involves the management of processes in a unified system. Logistics processes require efforts to be focused on the delivery of material flows by managing the selection and supplier performance improvement to just-in-time delivery of goods and customer service.

An important condition for the measurement and analysis of quality in logistics is the determination of the appropriate attributes for its measurement and their respective weights in the complex assessment. A review of the more common attributes in the scientific literature is made, highlighting that delivery time is the most used metric and delivery delays are the most common cause of deteriorating customer satisfaction. A critical review of the main models for assessing logistics service quality is provided.

The main aspects of logistics risk management are discussed. It is found that risk reduction opportunities depend on multiple interrelated factors and each of them can be the cause of drastic risk reduction if used wisely. It focuses on the four stages that should be followed as a continuous process to minimize the negative impact of risks and identify opportunities for improvement.

Risk management in logistics and supply chains has been studied by many researchers. Their results confirm that mitigation opportunities depend on multiple interrelated factors and each of them can be the cause of drastic risk reduction if used wisely. These major risks can be managed if, based on the cause-effect relationships between different factors, work is done to reduce the overall impact of the risk.

The study focuses on the integration of quality and risk management in the supply chain to examine the theoretical and practical guidelines and address the main risks of non-compliance with the customer and legislative requirements that arise in a constantly changing external environment.

Author details

Marieta Stefanova
Department of Management and Logistics, Nikola Vaptsarov Naval Academy, Varna, Bulgaria

*Address all correspondence to: m.stefanova@nvna.eu

References

[1] Team TNCPERE. The epidemiological characteristics of an outbreak of 2019 novel Coronavirus diseases (COVID-19)—China, 2020. China CDC Weekly. 2020;**2**:113-122

[2] World Health Organization. Clinical management of severe acute respiratory infection when novel coronavirus (2019-nCoV) infection is suspected: Interim guidance. In: Clinical Management of Severe Acute Respiratory Infection When Novel Coronavirus (2019-NCoV) Infection Is Suspected: Interim Guidance 2020. Geneva, Switzerland: World Health Organization; 2020

[3] World Health Organization. Rational Use of Personal Protective Equipment for Coronavirus Disease (COVID-19): Interim Guidance, 2020. Geneva, Switzerland: World Health Organization; 2020

[4] World Health Organization. Looking back at a year that changed the world: WHO's response to COVID-19, 2021. Geneva, Switzerland: World Health Organization; 2021

[5] Rajan SI, Cherian AP. COVID-19: Urban vulnerability and the need for transformations. Environment and Urbanization ASIA. 2021;**12**:310-322. DOI: 10.1177/09754253211040195

[6] Nicola M, Alsafi Z, Sohrabi C, Kerwan A, Al-Jabir A, Iosifidis C, et al. The socio-economic implications of the coronavirus pandemic (COVID-19): A review. International Journal of Surgery. 2020;**78**:185-193. DOI: 10.1016/j.ijsu.2020.04.018

[7] Canhoto AI, Wei L. Stakeholders of the world, unite!: Hospitality in the time of COVID-19. International Journal of Hospitality Management. 2021;**95**:102922. DOI: 10.1016/j.ijhm.2021.102922

[8] Yu Z. Disruption in global supply chain and socio-economic shocks: A lesson from COVID-19 for sustainable production and consumption. Operations Management Research. 2021;**4549**:1-16

[9] Prokopowicz D, Gołębiowska A. Increase in the Internetization of Economic Processes, Economic, Pandemic and Climate Crisis as Well as Cybersecurity as Key Challenges and Philosophical Paradigms for the Development of the 21st Century Civilization. 2021.

[10] Prokopowicz D, Gołębiowska A. Business Intelligence Analytics Based on the Processing of Large Sets of Information with the Use of Sentiment Analysis and Big Data. Warsaw: SGSP; 2021. pp. 129-154

[11] Cohen J, van der Rodgers YM. Contributing factors to personal protective equipment shortages during the COVID-19 pandemic. Preventive Medicine. Elsevier. 2020;**141**:106263. DOI: 10.1016/j.ypmed.2020.106263

[12] Tisdell CA. Economic, social and political issues raised by the COVID-19 pandemic. Economic Analysis and Policy. 2020;**68**:17-28. DOI: 10.1016/j.eap.2020.08.002

[13] Aleksandrov I, Arnaudova M, Stoyanov V, Ivanova V, Petrov PY. On psychological and psychiatric impact of piracy on seafarers. Journal of IMAB – Annual Proceeding Scientific Papers. 2015;**21**:991-994. DOI: 10.5272/jimab.2015214.991

[14] Prokopowicz D, Gołębiowska A. The Impact of the SARS-CoV-2 (COVID-19) coronavirus pandemic on ecological security and the development of international environmental policy. Zeszyty Naukowe SGSP. 2021;**80**(2):179-212

[15] United Nations. Coronavirus. New York, New York, United States: United Nations; 2021

[16] Choi T. Innovative "bring-service-near-your-home" operations under corona-virus (COVID-19/SARS-CoV-2) outbreak: Can logistics become the messiah? Transportation Research Part E: Logistics and Transportation Review. 2020;**101961**:140

[17] Mollenkopf DA, Ozanne LK, Stolze HJ. A transformative supply chain response to COVID-19. Journal of Service Management. 2020;**32**:190-202. DOI: 10.1108/JOSM-05-2020-0143

[18] Ikram M, Shen Y, Ferasso M, D'Adamo I. Intensifying effects of COVID-19 on economic growth, logistics performance, environmental sustainability and quality management: Evidence from Asian countries. JABS. 2021:1-24. DOI: 10.1108/JABS-07-2021-0316. [ahead-of-print]

[19] Atayah OF, Dhiaf MM, Najaf K, Frederico GF. Impact of COVID-19 on financial performance of logistics firms: Evidence from G-20 countries. JGOSS. 2021. DOI: 10.1108/JGOSS-03-2021-0028. [ahead-of-print]

[20] Regal Ludowieg A, Ortega C, Bronfman A, Rodriguez Serra M, Chong M. A methodology for managing public spaces to increase access to essential goods and services by vulnerable populations during the COVID-19 pandemic. Journal of Humanitarian Logistics and Supply Chain Management. 2021. DOI: 10.1108/JHLSCM-02-2021-0012. [ahead-of-print]

[21] Fedotova I, Dimitrakieva S, Shynkarenko V, Kryvoruchko O, Shynkarenko V, Bocharova N. Using the elements from a fuzzy sets theory in the process of diagnosing the loyalty of consumers of motor transport services. Eastern-European Journal of Enterprise Technologies. 2019;**3**:39-49. DOI: 10.15587/1729-4061.2019.169079

[22] Loxton M, Truskett R, Scarf B, Sindone L, Baldry G, Zhao Y. Consumer behaviour during crises: Preliminary research on how Coronavirus has manifested consumer panic buying, herd mentality, Changing discretionary spending and the role of the media in influencing behaviour. Journal of Risk and Financial Management. 2020;**13**:166. DOI: 10.3390/jrfm13080166

[23] Stoyanov V. Coping with stress at different levels of work stress. Journal VFU. 2011:1-15

[24] Mostafa N, Galal A, Elawady H. A proposed approach for selecting third party logistic alternatives. Egyptian Journal for Engineering Sciences and Technology. 2021;**35**:48-56. DOI: 10.21608/eijest.2021.48088.1023

[25] Choi T. Risk analysis in logistics systems: A research agenda during and after the COVID-19 pandemic. Transportation Research Part E: Logistics and Transportation Review. 2020;**145**:102190

[26] Laila A. Impact of COVID-19 on food waste behaviour of families: Results from household waste composition audits. Socio-Economic Planning Sciences. 2021:101188

[27] Gu S, Ślusarczyk B, Hajizada S, Kovalyova I. Impact of the COVID-19

pandemic on online consumer purchasing behavior. Journal of Theoretical and Applied Electronic Commerce Research. 2021;**16**:2263-2281. DOI: 10.3390/jtaer16060125

[28] Stoyanov V. Live through of the students in the conditions of pandemic of COVID-19. Strategies for Policy in Science and Education-Strategii Na Obrazovatelnata I Nauchnata Politika. 2021;**29**:154-171. DOI: 10.53656/str2021-2-3-pan

[29] Puram P, Gurumurthy A, Narmetta M, Mor R. Last-mile challenges in on-demand food delivery during COVID-19: Understanding the riders' perspective using a grounded theory approach. The International Journal of Logistics Management. 2021. DOI: 10.1108/IJLM-01-2021-0024. [ahead-of-print]

[30] Singh S, Kumar R, Panchal R, Tiwari M. Impact of COVID-19 on logistics systems and disruptions in food supply chain. International Journal of Production Research. 2021;**59**:1993-2008

[31] Butt A. Supply chains and COVID-19: Impacts, countermeasures and post-COVID-19 era. The International Journal of Logistics Management. 2021. DOI: 10.1108/IJLM-02-2021-0114. [ahead-of-print]

[32] Dimitrakieva S, Kostadinov O, Atanasova K. Comparative analysis of the contracts for maritime transport services; chain of charter parties. Pedagogika-Pedagogy. 2021;**93**:51-62. DOI: 10.53656/ped21-6s.04com

[33] Thabah A, Suyono E, Anggraeni A, Kaukab M. A new challenge of supply chain in emergency response management: A case study of Covid-19 pandemic. Turkish Journal of Computer and Mathematics Education. 2021;**12**:4778-4791

[34] Badraoui I, Boulaksil Y, Vorst JGAJ van der. A typology of horizontal logistics collaboration concepts: An illustrative case study from agri-food supply chains. Benchmarking 2021. pp. 1-27. DOI: 10.1108/BIJ-02-2021-0082. [ahead-of-print]

[35] Badraoui I, van der Lans I, Boulaksil Y, van der Vorst JGAJ. Antecedents of horizontal logistics collaboration in agri-food supply chains. The International Journal of Logistics Management. 2021;**33**(1):239-260. DOI: 10.1108/IJLM-09-2020-0362

[36] Lotfi M, Larmour A. Supply chain resilience in the face of uncertainty: How horizontal and vertical collaboration can help? Continuity & Resilience Review. 2021. DOI: 10.1108/CRR-04-2021-0016. [ahead-of-print]

[37] Jha SK. Imperatives for open innovation in times of COVID-19. International Journal of Innovation Science. 2021. [ahead-of-print]

[38] Shanker S. Enhancing resiliency of perishable product supply chains in the context of the COVID-19 outbreak. International Journal of Logistics Research and Applications. 2021:1-25. DOI: 10.1080/13675567.2021.1893671. [Published online: 02 Mar 2021]

[39] Radev R, Pashova S. Application of Edible Films and Coatings for Fresh Fruit and Vegetables 2020. Available from: https://scholar.google.bg/citations?view_op=view_citation&hl=bg&user=bQ12nJ0AAAAJ&alert_preview_top_rm=2&citation_for_view=bQ12nJ0AAAAJ:hMod-77fHWUC [Accessed: January 11, 2022]

[40] Das D. Building supply chain resilience in the era of COVID-19. Operations Management Research. June 2021;**21**:1-19

[41] Montoya-Torres J, Muñoz-Villamizar A, Mejia-Argueta C. Mapping research in logistics and supply chain management during COVID-19 pandemic. International Journal of Logistics Research and Applications. 2021:1-21. DOI: 10.1080/13675567.2021.1958768. [Published online: 26 Jul 2021] [Epub ahead of print]

[42] Mishra R, Singh R, Subramanian N. Impact of disruptions in agri-food supply chain due to COVID-19 pandemic: Contextualized resilience framework to achieve operational excellence. The International Journal of Logistics Management. 2021. DOI: 10.1108/IJLM-01-2021-0043. [ahead-of-print]

[43] Rajak S. Issues and analysis of critical success factors for the sustainable initiatives in the supply chain during COVID-19 pandemic outbreak in India: A case study. Research in Transportation Economics. 2021;**101114** DOI: 10.1016/j.retrec.2021.101114

[44] Dimitrakieva S. An approach for forming the brand communication strategy. Analele Universitatii Maritime Constanta. 2014;**15**:139-144

[45] Dimitrakieva S. Analysis of the practical methods for brand positioning. Bulletin of Perm National Research Polytechnic University. Social and Economic Sciences. 2015;**1**:49-56

[46] Gronroos C. Service quality: The six criteria of good perceived service. Review of Business. 1988;**9**:10-15

[47] Christopher M. Logistics and Supply Chain Management. 1st ed. London: Financial Times/Irwin Professional Publications; 1992

[48] Limbourg S, Giang H, Cools M. Logistics service quality: The case of Da Nang city. Procedia Engineering. 2016;**142**:124-130

[49] Dimitrakieva S. Brand Image and its Exploration. Paris, France: Innovative Development of the Economy: Trends and Prospects; 2015

[50] Dimitrakieva S. Brand Value–How to Evaluate? Perm: Bulletin of the Perm National Research Polytechnic University Social and Economic Sciences; 2014

[51] Dimitrakieva S, Kostadinov O, Atanasova K. Multilevel demand for sea transportation; correlation between Baltic dry index (BDI) and coaster shipping prices for sea routes between Baltic seaports and Mediterranean seaports. Pedagogika-Pedagogy. 2021;**93**:141-148. DOI: 10.53656/ped21-7s.12corr

[52] Gagliano B, Hathcote J. Customer expectations and perceptions of service quality in retail apparel specialty stores. Journal of Services Marketing. 1994;**8**:60-69. DOI: 10.1108/08876049410053311

[53] Brogowicz A, Delene L, Lyth D. A synthesised service quality model with managerial implications. International Journal of Service Industry Management. 1990;**1**:1-10. DOI: 10.1108/09564239010001640

[54] Carman JM. Consumer perceptions of service quality: An assessment of T. Journal of Retailing. 1990;**66**:33

[55] Bandittayarak H et al. Improving performance, logistics service quality to further enhance the create competitive advantage of logistics service providers: Container road transportation. Psychology and Education Journal. 2021;**58**:3883-3891

[56] Chandra C, Kumar S. Supply chain management in theory and practice: A passing fad or a fundamental change? Industrial Management & Data Systems. 2000;**100**:100-114 10.1108/02635570010286168

[57] Daugherty PJ, Ellinger AE, Gustin CM. Integrated logistics: Achieving logistics performance improvements. Supply Chain Management. 1996;**1**:25-33. DOI: 10.1108/13598549610155297

[58] Saura IG, Francés DS, Contri GB, Blasco MF. Logistics service quality: A new way to loyalty. Industrial Management & Data Systems. 2008;**108**:650-668 10.1108/02635570810876778

[59] Werbińska-Wojciechowska S. On logistics service quality evaluation-case study. Logistics and Transport. 2011;**13**:45-56

[60] Zaitova A. Logistics management. Crisis and Risk Engineering for Transport Services. 2021;**1**(1)::383-388

[61] Islam DMZ, Fabian Meier J, Aditjandra PT, Zunder TH, Pace G. Logistics and supply chain management. Research in Transportation Economics. 2013;**41**:3-16. DOI: 10.1016/j.retrec.2012.10.006

[62] Rauyruen P, Miller KE. Relationship quality as a predictor of B2B customer loyalty. Journal of Business Research. 2007;**60**:21-31. DOI: 10.1016/j.jbusres.2005.11.006

[63] Vunova K. Relation entrepreneurial culture–organisational culture. The Process of Business Development Revista Economica. 2009;**46**:158-169

[64] Kanev D, Toncheva S, Terziev V, Narleva K. Specific Aspects of Motivation of Seafarers. Social Science Research Network: Rochester, NY; 2017. DOI: 10.2139/ssrn.3144743. Available from: https://web.archive.org/web/20220111123810/https://papers.ssrn.com/sol3/papers.cfm?abstract_id=3144743

[65] Chen KK, Chang CT, Lai CS. Service quality gaps of business customers in the shipping industry. Transportation Research Part E: Logistics and Transportation Review. 2009;**45**:222-237. DOI: 10.1016/j.tre.2008.02.005

[66] Huang B, Wang T, Xue X. Service-selecting approach based on domain-specified "quality of service" model and its application in logistics. The Service Industries Journal. 2012;**32**:1571-1588. DOI: 10.1080/02642069.2010.551761

[67] Parasuraman A, Zeithaml VA, Berry LL. A conceptual model of service quality and its implications for future research. Journal of Marketing. 1985;**49**:41-50

[68] Xu J, Cao Z. Logistics service quality analysis based on gray correlation method. International Journal of Business and Management. 2008;**3**:58-61

[69] Mentzer J, Flint D, Hult G. Logistics service quality as a segment-customized process. Journal of Marketing. 2001;**65**: 82-104. DOI: 10.1509/jmkg.65.4.82.18390

[70] Qin Q. Research on logistics service quality evaluation indexes of automobile special steel of BJ company. Otago University Research Archive. 2021;**1**:1-266

[71] Gupta A, Singh R, Suri P. Sustainable service quality management by logistics service providers: An Indian perspective. Global Business Review. 2018;**19**:130-150

[72] Kilibarda M, Nikolicic S, Andrejic M. Measurement of logistics service quality in freight forwarding companies: A case study of the Serbian market. The International Journal of Logistics Management. 2016;**27**:770-794. DOI: 10.1108/IJLM-04-2014-0063

[73] Stoykova T, Zlateva D, Pashova S. Commodity science in modern market conditions. In: Economic Science,

Education and the Real Economy: Development and Interactions in the Digital Age. Varna: Publishing House Science and Economics; 2020

[74] Thai V. Logistics service quality: Conceptual model and empirical evidence. International Journal of Logistics Research and Applications. 2013;**16**:114-131. DOI: 10.1080/13675567.2013.804907

[75] Uvet H, Uvet H. Importance of logistics service quality in customer satisfaction: An empirical study. Operations and Supply Chain Management: An International Journal. 2020;**13**:1-10. DOI: 10.31387/oscm0400248

[76] Panayides P, So M. The impact of integrated logistics relationships on third-party logistics service quality and performance. Maritime Economics & Logistics. 2005;7:36-55. DOI: 10.1057/palgrave.mel.9100123

[77] Bouzaabia R, Bouzaabia O, Capatina A. Retail logistics service quality: A cross-cultural survey on customer perceptions. International Journal of Retail & Distribution Management. 2013;**41**:627-647. DOI: 10.1108/IJRDM-02-2012-0012

[78] Bienstock CC, Royne MB, Sherrell D, Stafford TF. An expanded model of logistics service quality: Incorporating logistics information technology. International Journal of Production Economics. 2008;**113**:205-222. DOI: 10.1016/j.ijpe.2007.03.023

[79] Gil-Saura I, Ruiz-Molina M. Logistics service quality and buyer–customer relationships: The moderating role of technology in B2B and B2C contexts. The Service Industries Journal. 2011;**3**:1109-1123. DOI: 10.1080/02642060903100380

[80] Feng Y, Zheng B, Tan J. Exploratory study of logistics service quality scale based on online shopping malls. Journal of Zhejiang University-Science A. 2007;**8**:926-931. DOI: 10.1631/jzus.2007.A0926

[81] Widiyanto P. The relationship between service quality, timeliness of arrival, departure flip ship logistics and people and customer satisfaction: A case in Indonesia. Academy of Entrepreneurship Journal. 2021;**27**:1-12

[82] Chen S, Wang Y, Han S, Lim M. Evaluation of fresh food logistics service quality using online customer reviews. International Journal of Logistics Research and Applications. 2021;**1**:1-17

[83] Arabelen G, Kaya HT. Assessment of logistics service quality dimensions: A qualitative approach. Journal of Shipping and Trade. 2021;**6**:14. DOI: 10.1186/s41072-021-00095-1

[84] Dimitrakieva S, Koritarov AK. The human element as a factor for sustainable development of the offshore oil industry. Scientific Works - Naval University N Y Vaptsarov. 2018;**32**:65-68

[85] Zhang O, Vonderembse M, Lim J. Logistics flexibility and its impact on customer satisfaction. The International Journal of Logistics Management. 2005;**16**:71-95. DOI: 10.1108/09574090510617367

[86] Zhang Q, Vonderembse MA, Lim J-S. Spanning flexibility: Supply chain information dissemination drives strategy development and customer satisfaction. Supply Chain Management: An International Journal. 2006;**11**(5):390-399. DOI: 10.1108/13598540610682408

[87] Stopka O, Černá L, Zitrický V. Methodology for measuring the customer satisfaction with the logistics services. NAŠE MORE: Znanstveni Časopis Za More i Pomorstvo. 2016;**63**:189-194

[88] Kearney AT. Achieving customer satisfaction through logistics excellence. Managing Service Quality. 1994;**4**:47-50. DOI: 10.1108/09604529410796224

[89] Novack R, Rinehart L, Langley J. An internal assessment of logistics value. Journal of Business Logistics. 1994;**15**:113

[90] Kilibarda M, Andrejić M, Popović V. Creating and measuring logistics value. In: 1st Logistics International Conference. Belgrade, Serbia: LOGIC; 2013. pp. 197-202

[91] Giannikas V, McFarlane D. Examining the value of flexible logistics offerings. European Journal of Operational Research. 2021;**290**:968-981. DOI: 10.1016/j.ejor.2020.08.056

[92] Shah T, Sharma M. Comprehensive view of logistics flexibility and its impact on customer satisfaction. International Journal of Logistics Systems and Management. 2014;**19**:43-61. DOI: 10.1504/IJLSM.2014.064030

[93] Jafari H. Logistics flexibility: A systematic review. International Journal of Productivity and Performance Management. 2015;**64**:947-970. DOI: 10.1108/IJPPM-05-2014-0069

[94] Hartmann E, de Grahl A. The flexibility of logistics service providers and its impact on customer loyalty—An empirical study. In: Success Factors in Logistics Outsourcing. Wiesbaden: Gabler Verlag; 2011. pp. 7-51. DOI: 10.1007/978-3-8349-7084-8_2. Available from: https://web.archive.org/web/20220109005908/https://link.springer.com/chapter/10.1007%2F978-3-8349-7084-8_2

[95] Yu Y, Huo B. Supply chain quality integration: Relational antecedents and operational consequences. Supply Chain Management. 2018;**23**:188-206. DOI: 10.1108/SCM-08-2017-0280

[96] Huma S, Ahmed W, Ikram M, Khawaja MI. The effect of logistics service quality on customer loyalty: Case of logistics service industry. SAJBS. 2019;**9**:43-61. DOI: 10.1108/SAJBS-10-2018-0114

[97] Nordås H, Pinali E, Grosso M. Logistics and time as a trade barrier. OECD Trade Policy Papers. 2006;**35**:1-59. DOI: 10.1787/664220308873

[98] Lim M, Li Y, Song X. Exploring customer satisfaction in cold chain logistics using a text mining approach. Industrial Management & Data Systems. 2021;**121**:2426-2449. DOI: 10.1108/IMDS-05-2021-0283

[99] Sarder M. Logistics customer services. Logistics Transportation Systems. 2021;**10**:197-217. DOI: 10.1016/B978-0-12-815974-3.00008-3

[100] Lemke J, Kijewska K, Iwan S, Dudek T. Six sigma in urban logistics management—A case study. Sustainability. 2021;**13**:4302. DOI: 10.3390/su13084302

[101] Tian Z. A blockchain-based evaluation approach for customer delivery satisfaction in sustainable urban logistics. International Journal of Production Research. 2021;**59**:2229-2249. DOI: 10.1080/00207543.2020.1809733

[102] Mehrolia S, Alagarsamy S, Solaikutty V. Customers response to online food delivery services during COVID-19 outbreak using binary logistic regression. International Journal of Consumer Studies. 2021;**45**:396-408. DOI: 10.1111/ijcs.12630

[103] Tersine R, Hummingbird E. Lead-time reduction: The search for competitive advantage. International Journal of Operations & Production Management. 1995;**15**:8-18. DOI: 10.1108/01443579510080382

[104] Kuhlang P, Edtmayr T, Sihn W. Methodical approach to increase productivity and reduce lead time in assembly and production-logistic processes. CIRP Journal of Manufacturing Science and Technology. 2011;**4**:24-32. DOI: 10.1016/j.cirpj.2011.02.001

[105] Closs D, Goldsby T, Clinton S. Information technology influences on world class logistics capability. International Journal of Physical Distribution & Logistics Management. 1997;**27**:4-17. DOI: 10.1108/09600039710162259

[106] Dai M, Xu R, Du J, Liu Y, Xing H. Network characteristics and risk analysis of logistics sharing economy. In: 2021 4th international Conference on Artificial Intelligence and Big Data (ICAIBD). London: IEEE; 2021. pp. 594-598. DOI: 10.1109/ICAIBD51990.2021.9458973

[107] Bihua Y et al. The study of logistics service guarantee and purchase intention in the context of E-commerce. International Journal of Science and Business. 2021;**5**:29-45

[108] Karcz J, Ślusarczyk B. Criteria of quality requirements deciding on choice of the logistic operator from a perspective of his customer and the end recipient of goods. Production Engineering Archives. 2021;**27**:58-68. DOI: 10.30657/pea.2021.27.8

[109] Dullaert W, Zamparini L. The impact of lead time reliability in freight transport: A logistics assessment of transport economics findings. Transportation Research Part E: Logistics and Transportation Review. 2013;**49**: 190-200. DOI: 10.1016/j.tre.2012.08.005

[110] Das R, Hanaoka S. Relief inventory modelling with stochastic lead-time and demand. European Journal of Operational Research. 2014;**235**:616-623. DOI: 10.1016/j.ejor.2013.12.042

[111] Kamble SS, Raut R, Dhume S. Validating the logistics service quality (LSQ) scale in Indian logistics industry. International Conference on Business and Economics Research. 2011;**1**:81-85

[112] Gupta A, Singh R, Mangla S. Evaluation of logistics providers for sustainable service quality: Analytics based decision making framework. Annals of Operations Research. 2021;**1**:1-48

[113] Li S, Lin B. Accessing information sharing and information quality in supply chain management. Decision Support Systems. 2006;**42**:1641-1656. DOI: 10.1016/j.dss.2006.02.011

[114] Li X. What influences panic buying behaviour? A model based on dual-system theory and stimulus-organism-response framework. International Journal of Disaster Risk Reduction. 2021;**64**:102484

[115] Dimitrakiev D, Molodchik A. Digital platforms as factor transforming management models in businesses and industries. In: Journal of Physics: Conference Series. Vol. 1015. Bristol, United Kingdom: IOP Publishing; 2018. p. 042040. DOI: 10.1088/1742-6596/1015/4/042040

[116] Otsetova A. Validation of the logistics service quality scale in Bulgarian courier sector. Management & Education/Upravlenie i Obrazovanie. 2016;**12**:46-52

[117] Richey R, Daugherty P, Roath A. Firm technological readiness and complementarity: Capabilities impacting logistics service competency and performance. Journal of Business Logistics. 2007;**28**:195-228. DOI: 10.1002/j.2158-1592.2007.tb00237.x

[118] Toufik I, Qamari I. Logistics service quality as mediation of the effect of information systems on supply chain relationship. In: 4th International Conference on Sustainable Innovation 2020-Accounting and Management (ICoSIAMS 2020). Berlin: Atlantis Press. pp. 44-49

[119] Sutrisno A, Andajani E, Widjaja F. The effects of service quality on customer satisfaction and loyalty in a logistics company. KnE Social Sciences. 2019;**2019**:85-92

[120] Parasuraman A, Zeithaml V, Berry L. Reassessment of expectations as a comparison standard in measuring service quality: Implications for further research. Journal of Marketing. 1994;**58**:111-124

[121] Parasuraman A, Zeithaml V, Berry L. SERVQUAL: A multiple-item scale for measuring consumer perceptions of service quality. Journal of Retailing. 1988;**64**:12-40

[122] Choy K. Managing uncertainty in logistics service supply chain. International Journal of Risk Assessment and Management. 2007;**7**:19-43. DOI: 10.1504/IJRAM.2007.011408

[123] Weng J. Exploration of innovative development of logistics management in the Internet age. In: Kacprzyk J, editor. International Conference on Applications and Techniques in Cyber Security and Intelligence. Cham: Springer; 2021. pp. 173-179

[124] Grönroos C. A service quality model and its marketing implications. European Journal of Marketing. 1984;**18**:36-44. DOI: 10.1108/EUM0000000004784

[125] Ghotbabadi A, Baharun R, Feiz S. A review of service quality models. In: 2nd International Conference on Management. 2nd International Conference on Management. Malaysia: University Technology Malaysia; 2012. pp. 1-8

[126] Kang G, James J. Service quality dimensions: An examination of Grönroos's service quality model. Managing Service Quality: An International Journal. 2004;**14**:266-277. DOI: 10.1108/09604520410546806

[127] Rahman M, Khan A, Haque M. A conceptual study on the relationship between service quality towards customer satisfaction: Servqual and Gronroos's service quality model perspective. Asian Social Science. 2012;**8**:201. DOI: 10.5539/ass.v8n13p201

[128] Zaibaf M, Taherikia F, Fakharian M. Effect of perceived service quality on customer satisfaction in hospitality industry: Gronroos' service quality model development. Journal of Hospitality Marketing & Management. 2013;**22**:490-504. DOI: 10.1080/19368623.2012.670893

[129] Juhl HJ, Kristensen K, Østergaard P. Customer satisfaction in European food retailing. Journal of Retailing and Consumer Services. 2002;**9**:327-334. DOI: 10.1016/S0969-6989(02)00014-0

[130] Selivanova I, Hallissey A, Letsios A, Eklöf J. The EPSI rating initiative. European Quality. 2002;**9**:10-25

[131] Hallencreutz J, Parmler J. Important drivers for customer satisfaction—From product focus to image and service quality. Total Quality Management & Business Excellence. 2021;**32**:501-510. DOI: 10.1080/14783363.2019.1594756

[132] Mangla S. Total quality management (TQM): Principles, methods. Leadership & Organization Development Journal. 2021;**13**:3-7

[133] Fornell C, Cha J. Partial Least Squares. In: Bagozzi RP, Editor. Advanced Methods of Marketing Research. 1st ed. Cambridge: Blackwell; 1994

[134] Fornell C, Johnson MD, Anderson EW, Cha J, Bryant BE. The American customer satisfaction index: Nature, purpose, and findings. Journal of Marketing. 1996;**60**:7-18

[135] Anderson EW, Fornell C. Foundations of the American customer satisfaction index. Total Quality Management. 2000;**11**:869-882. DOI: 10.1080/09544120050135425

[136] Grigoroudis E, Siskos Y. A survey of customer satisfaction barometers: Some results from the transportation-communications sector. European Journal of Operational Research. 2004;**15**:334-353. DOI: 10.1016/S0377-2217(03)00028-6

[137] Kristensen K, Martensen A, Gronholdt L. Customer satisfaction measurement at post Denmark: Results of application of the European customer satisfaction index methodology. Total Quality Management. 2000;**11**:1007-1015. DOI: 10.1080/09544120050135533

[138] Gronholdt L, Martensen A, Kristensen K. The relationship between customer satisfaction and loyalty: Cross-industry differences. Total Quality Management. 2000;**11**:509-514. DOI: 10.1080/09544120050007823

[139] Arvis J. Connecting to Compete 2018: Trade Logistics in the Global Economy. 1st ed. World Bank: Washington; 2018

[140] Curry A. Innovation in public service management. Managing Service Quality: An International Journal. 1999;**9**:180-190. DOI: 10.1108/09604529910267082

[141] Rajesh R, Ravi V. Modeling enablers of supply chain risk mitigation in electronic supply chains. A Grey–DEMA^{TEL} approach. Computers & Industrial Engineering. 2015;**87**:126-139. DOI: 10.1016/j.cie.2015.04.028

[142] Tang CS. Perspectives in supply chain risk management. International Journal of Production Economics. 2006;**103**:451-488. DOI: 10.1016/j.ijpe.2005.12.006

[143] Olson D, Wu D. Supply Chain Risk Management. New Frontiers in Enterprise Risk Management. 1st ed. Berlin, Heidelberg: Springer; 2008

[144] Cagliano AC, De Marco A, Grimaldi S, Rafele C. An integrated approach to supply chain risk analysis. Journal of Risk Research. 2012;**15**:817-840. DOI: 10.1080/13669877.2012.666757

[145] Barnes-Schuster D, Bassok Y, Anupindi R. Coordination and flexibility in supply contracts with options. M&SOM. 2002;**4**:171-207. DOI: 10.1287/msom.4.3.171.7754

[146] Tsay AA, Lovejoy WS. Quantity flexibility contracts and supply chain performance. Manufacturing & Service Operations Management. 1999;**1**:89-111. DOI: 10.1287/msom.1.2.89

[147] Tang C, Tomlin B. The power of flexibility for mitigating supply chain risks. International Journal of Production Economics. 2008;**116**:12-27. DOI: 10.1016/j.ijpe.2008.07.008

[148] Tang O, Musa S. Identifying risk issues and research advancements in supply chain risk management. International Journal of Production Economics. 2011;**133**:25-34. DOI: 10.1016/j.ijpe.2010.06.013

[149] Fuchs H, Wohinz J. Risk management in logistics systems. Advances in Production Engineering & Management. 2009;**4**:233-242

[150] Garvey M, Carnovale S, Yeniyurt S. An analytical framework for supply network risk propagation: A Bayesian network approach. European Journal of Operational Research. 2015;**242**:618-627. DOI: 10.1016/j.ejor.2014.10.034

[151] Marinova V, Stoyanova A. Paper recycling in Covid-19 conditions. Izvestia Journal of the Union of Scientists-Varna Economic Sciences Series. 2020;**9**:43-52

[152] Gallucci T, Lagioia G, Dimitrova V, Marinov S, Amicarelli V, Vassileva B, et al. Theory and Practice of Circular Economy. Sofia: Direct Services; 2019. p. 306

[153] Essaber FE, Benmoussa R, De Guio R, Dubois S. A hybrid supply chain risk management approach for lean green performance based on AHP. RCA and TRIZ: A Case Study. Sustainability. 2021;**13**:8492. DOI: 10.3390/su13158492

[154] Kirechev D. Improving access to finance for agricultural HOLDINDS as a factor for the sustainability of agricultural financing in Bulgaria. Trakia Journal of Sciences. 2021;**19**:197-206. DOI: 10.15547/tjs.2021.s.01.030

[155] Xu W, Zhang Z, Gong D, Guan X. Neural network model for the risk prediction in cold chain logistics. International Journal of Multimedia and Ubiquitous Engineering. 2014;**9**:111-124. DOI: 10.14257/ijmue.2014.9.8.10

[156] Lai K, Vejvar M, Lun V. Risk in port logistics: Risk classification and mitigation framework. International Journal of Shipping and Transport Logistics. 2020;**12**:576-596

[157] Caunhye AM, Nie X, Pokharel S. Optimization models in emergency logistics: A literature review. Socio-Economic Planning Sciences. 2012;**46**: 4-13. DOI: 10.1016/j.seps.2011.04.004

[158] Marinova V, Stoyanova A, Radev R, Zhivkova V. Quality of goods and digital consumption-prospects and disadvantages. Economic Science, Education and the Real Economy: Development and Interactions in the Digital Age. 2020;**1**:693-706

[159] Shen C. A Bayesian networks approach to modeling financial risks of e-logistics investments. International Journal of Information Technology & Decision Making. 2009;**8**:711-726. DOI: 10.1142/S0219622009003594

[160] Narleva K, Narlev J. Entrepreneurial management in small and medium-sized enterprises in Bulgaria on the example of the plastics processing enterprises. Economics and Computer Science. 2018;**1**:34-41

[161] Narleva K. Entrepreneurship and human resource management: Approaches and paradigms. In: Sustainable Human Resource Management in the Contemporary Economic Reality. Basel, Switzerland: MDPI; 2019. pp. 60-69

[162] Shahbaz M, Rasi R, Ahmad M. A novel classification of supply chain risks: Scale development and validation. Journal of Industrial Engineering and Management. 2019;**12**:201-218. DOI: 10.3926/jiem.2792

[163] Mednikarov B. Current trends in the maritime profession and their implications for the maritime education. Proceedings of the International Association of Maritime Universities Conference. 2019;**1**:275-286

[164] Kanev D. External stimuli and internal motivation. Economy and Economic Theory: Problems and Interactions, Conference Proceedings. 2017;**1**:47-57

[165] Kanev D. Commitment as a constraint to the pursuit of self-interest. Economics. 2017;**1**:3-20

[166] DuHadway S, Carnovale S, Hazen B. Understanding risk management for intentional supply chain disruptions: Risk detection, risk mitigation, and risk recovery. Annals of Operations Research. 2019;**283**:179-198. DOI: 10.1007/s10479-017-2452-0

Chapter 2

Research Methodology for Quality and Risk Management in Logistics

Marieta Stefanova

Abstract

This chapter sees an appropriate approach to build a quality management model by managing the risk of nonconforming logistics activities that result from dynamic environmental changes and contingencies. Logistics management has the misconception that reducing complaints would increase satisfaction to the same extent. Models for positively influencing satisfaction should contain much more than one variable. The customer satisfaction model used in this chapter contains six latent variables: Logistics satisfaction survey; analysis of data from the survey to measure satisfaction with logistics services; chapter to analyze the risk of noncompliant processes in logistics services; survey data analysis to measure the risk of noncompliant processes in logistics services. FMEA analysis was used as a method to investigate the consequences of emerging risks by quantifying the severity, likelihood of occurrence, and detection of nonconforming logistics services that further generated the RPN. The main objective of this chapter is to define the research design and the methods of data collection and analysis.

Keywords: SERVQUA, satisfaction, FMEA method

1. Introduction

The present chapter uses the SERVQUA model to identify the gaps between customer satisfaction and the needs of logistics service users by determining the relationship between customer satisfaction and targeted actions to manage the risk of dissatisfaction by logistics service providers.

The essence of the methodology used is based on the following model assumptions:

- Expectations and perceptions of the logistics services studied must at least match to obtain a positive assessment of quality from users of the service.

- In cases where there is a discrepancy between the target and actual values of the surveyed services, the quality score will be negative.

- Based on strategic discrepancies between target and actual values (system discrepancies) in quality, the reasons for the insufficiency of the measured service quality values are analyzed.

Opportunities to identify discrepancies are related to:

- Customer perceptions: Mismatch between customer expectations and perceptions of the management of the service received in a real environment.
- Senior management perceptions: Mismatch between the perception of the service provider's senior management and customer expectations of the proposed service quality specifications.
- Process execution: Mismatch between service quality specifications and actual performance.
- Communication with customers: Inconsistency between the service and the message addressed to the customer about the service.

1.1 Methodology for measuring satisfaction with logistics services

The survey was first conducted as a pilot online survey to test the feasibility of the questionnaire from 1 December 2020 to 1 January 2021. The pilot survey covered 15 respondents who were mailed the evaluation questionnaire. The results of the pilot survey showed that all the respondents understood all the questions.

The baseline survey was conducted through a questionnaire and included a sample of 115 respondents, who were required to have experience in managing logistics processes. The survey was conducted from 15 February 2021 to 15 April 2021. A total of 105 questionnaires were collected, of which 100 were valid (5 of the questionnaires were not completed correctly and some of the questions had more than one answer), with a response rate of 95%. The survey was conducted directly through a telephone interview or internet communication depending on the suitability of the respondents. The valid questionnaires were collected from 52 logistics service providers and 48 customers.

1.2 Modeling the hypothesis

The model used to conduct the chapter on customer satisfaction with logistics services contains seven latent variables. The antecedents of logistics service satisfaction are customer expectations of logistics service, perceived quality, perceived value, and image. While the two indicators of the consequences of satisfaction are: nonconformities (complaints, returns) and loyalty.

The latent variables were defined using manifest variables appropriate for the purposes of this chapter and were measured in the survey. Associations between manifest and latent variables are described using a set of equations with unknown coefficients.

The following latent variables and hypotheses were investigated and analyzed in this chapter:

- Expectation: Two indicators were studied. Customer expectations related to logistics service culture. The manifestation of expectations depends on how customers perceive and interpret the factors influencing the formation of expectations. Various factors are under the control of the company and depend on the performance of logistics services, while others depend entirely on customer perceptions (psychological, cultural, and social). Therefore, the quality of feedback and personal contact with employees have the potential to create value and should be a priority. Sales staff need to understand customer perceptions before guiding them to the appropriate choice of product for order preparation. The indicator relates to the provision of a correct logistics service, the speed of response, and the ability of customer-facing staff to make timely decisions on the disposal of a nonconforming product.

The expectation hypothesis: Customers' expectations of the services have a positive impact on the quality of the service provided and an indirect positive impact on overall satisfaction.

- Quality: Five indicators of the expected quality of logistics services were studied. Logistics service quality is the extent to which the set of inherent service characteristics satisfies the requirements of customers and stakeholders[1].

The hypothesis (Quality) that logistics service quality has a priority and positive impact on overall satisfaction was tested during the data analysis.

- Value: Two indicators of perceived value were investigated. The perceived value of logistics services motivates the customer to tradeoff between the quality received versus the price paid to acquire the service. The service that customers receive at the time of purchase influences the perceived value.

The hypothesis (Value) that customer perceived value has a positive impact on overall satisfaction with logistics services was tested during the data analysis.

- Image: The indicator refers to the good reputation and image of the logistics company or the ability of the service provider to inspire trust and confidence. The positive impact of this factor is achieved by measuring satisfaction through various means that provide tangibility to the logistics service and service culture including tangible items relating to the facility, environment, and all types of hardware and equipment required to provide services.

The hypothesis (Image) that customers' perceived image positively impacts expectations, overall satisfaction, and loyalty for logistics services was tested during the data analysis of the chapter.

- Satisfaction: Three satisfaction indicators were studied. The satisfaction indicator is related to the customer's reaction to the comparison between the expected and actual experience of the logistics service. An essential condition for achieving good financial performance lies in finding a way to minimize the differences between the expected and actual experience of the logistics service.

- Complaints: Customer discrepancies (customer complaints) that arise while providing logistics services that are unfulfilled as expected or actual customer requirements. Complaints should be used to improve any process in which a nonconformance is identified.

---

[1] The definition of quality is adapted from Clause 3. ISO 9001:2015 Terms and definitions.

- Loyalty: Customer loyalty is the customer's positive attitude towards the logistics service provided because of factors that are significant to the customer.

The questionnaire required each survey participant to rate the margin of acceptability of the quality of logistics services on a 5-point scale (0 points – does not meet customer requirements and 5 points – fully meets and exceeds requirements. In cases where respondents' perceptions did not match the two extremes of the rating, they

Rate the statements on a 5-point scale: (1) completely disagree (2) disagree (3) hesitate (4) agree (5) completely agree

Indicator	**Questions to respondents**	**Evaluation**
Expectation	PLSE1. The knowledge and experience of the nominated contact person are sufficient to understand the problems encountered	1☐2☐ 3☐ 4☐5☐
	PLSE2. Problems arising are resolved by the designated contact person	1☐2☐ 3☐ 4☐5☐
Quality	PLSQ1. Ordering procedures are easy to use	1☐2☐ 3☐ 4☐5☐
	PLSQ2. Shipments rarely contain incorrect quantity	1☐2☐ 3☐ 4☐5☐
	PLSQ3. Supplies arrive on the promised delivery date	1☐2☐ 3☐ 4☐5☐
	PLSQ4. Shipments rarely contain defective products	1☐2☐ 3☐ 4☐5☐
	PLSQ5. The manner in which claims are settled is adequate	1☐2☐ 3☐ 4☐5☐
Value	PLSV1. Logistics services meet the requirements (specifications)	1☐2☐ 3☐ 4☐5☐
	PLSV1. Logistics services are reliable and on time	1☐2☐ 3☐ 4☐5☐
Image	PLSI1. Complaints are rarely due to the method of transportation	1☐2☐ 3☐ 4☐5☐
	PLSI2. No difficulties have ever arisen due to lack of availability	1☐2☐ 3☐ 4☐5☐
	PLSI3. The time between placing the order and receiving the delivery is short	1☐2☐ 3☐ 4☐5☐
	PLSI4. Product return procedures are easy to use	1☐2☐ 3☐ 4☐5☐

Rate the statements on a 5-point scale: (1) completely disagree (2) disagree (3) hesitate (4) agree (5) completely agree		
Indicator	**Questions to respondents**	**Evaluation**
	PLSI5. The resulting products are not normally crushed damaged	1☐2☐ 3☐ 4☐5☐
Satisfaction	PLSS1. Logistics services to meet your expectations in number and scope	1☐2☐ 3☐ 4☐5☐
	PLSS2. Selected logistics services are the right choice	1☐2☐ 3☐ 4☐5☐
	PLSS3. I am satisfied with the overall logistics service	1☐2☐ 3☐ 4☐5☐
Complaint	PLSC1. The corrective actions taken following complaints are adequate for the problem encountered	1☐2☐ 3☐ 4☐5☐
	PLSC2. Corrective actions taken following complaints are timely	1☐2☐ 3☐ 4☐5☐
Loyalty	PLSL1 I would recommend the logistics services used	1☐2☐ 3☐ 4☐5☐
	PLSL2 I would use logistics services in the long-term	1☐2☐ 3☐ 4☐5☐

Table 1.
Survey questionnaire.

could select any number between 1 and 5 to rate how strong their expectations and perceptions were. The accompanying instructions explicitly stated that the purpose of the survey was not to find acceptable or unacceptable responses but only to establish the exact numerical rating that reflected their opinion of the quality of the logistics service and their level of satisfaction as its users.

The survey questionnaire is shown in **Table 1**.

1.3 Model of the empirical study of customer satisfaction with logistics services

Tenenhaus and Michel's [1] study built based on the SERVQUA methodology provides the reference for the possible and expected model of interaction between the variables that would be obtained based on the results of the study (**Figure 1**).

The partial least squares modeling method was used to analyze the data obtained from the survey measuring the identified gaps between satisfaction and needs of the logistics service user customers. Multivariate analyses (partial least squares path-modeling [PLS-PM]) were performed to simultaneously assess the potential relationships between different logistics service quality and satisfaction indicators. An appropriate analysis method was selected after investigating a convenient tool to examine the multiple relationships (latent variables) of variables (factors).

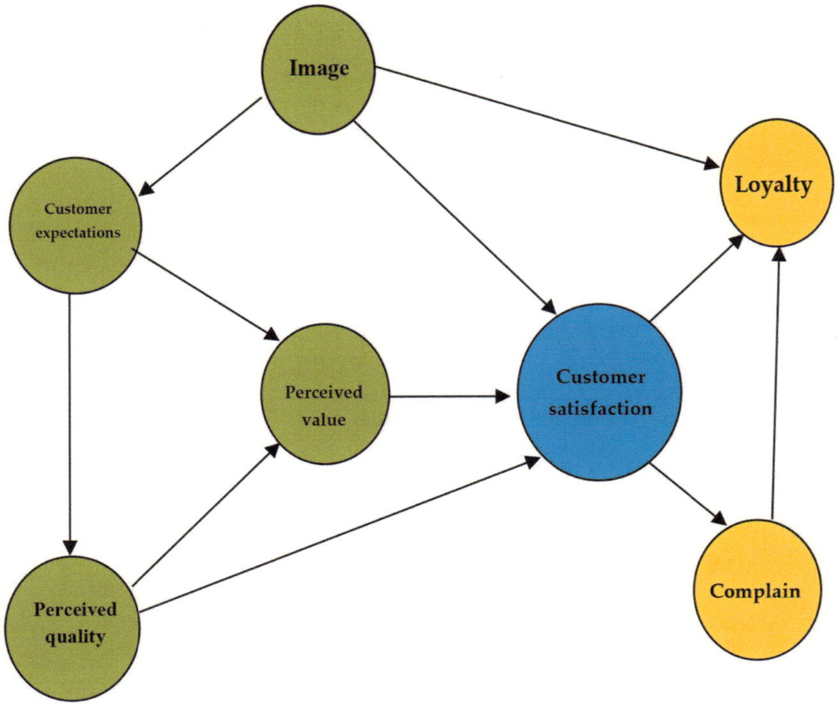

Figure 1.
Key attributes of the causal model describe the causes and consequences of customer satisfaction. Source [1].

1.3.1 Partial least squares path-Modeling (PLS-PM)

The PLS-PM model reflects causal relationships with arrows that start in a latent variable (factor) and point to measured indicator variables. The PLS-PM was chosen as the most convenient tool to examine relationships between observed and unobserved (latent) variables. Matrices in which 15–20% of the data are missing or have experimental errors can be processed by the PLS-PM method.

The possible outcomes of the PLS-PM study are presented in **Table 2.**

Through the assessment method, the relationship between variables acting on a particular outcome through multiple causal pathways is examined. Data processing was done using XLSTAT software [2] for modeling PLS relationships (pathways) implemented in the XLSTAT statistical analysis package of Microsoft Excel. The built-in XLSTAT-PLSPM interface [2] allows to build of a graphical representation of the model and to display results in Excel as tables or graphical images. XLSTAT-PLSPM is fully integrated with the XLSTAT package and allows different survey data analyses to be performed with other XLSTAT applications.

2. Methodology for conducting the risk analysis study of noncompliant processes in logistics services

The main objective of the risk analysis of noncompliant processes in logistics services is to identify, assess, and forecast the significant factors that affect the

Indication of the indicator	Interpretation of the result
	Apparent (observed) variable Observed variables are measured directly and reflect data on the process under study.
	Latent (unobserved) variable The latent variables cannot be measured directly and, accordingly, we make assumptions about the expected influence on the observed variables through modeling.
R^2	The values for this indicator show the amount of variation in the dependent variable resulting from the influence of the independent latent variables. When the values are above 0.5, the dependence is considered to be large.
Path coefficient (β)	Standardized direct and indirect mean effects derived from partial least squares modeling. Path coefficients between latent variables range between −1 and + 1. The closer the indicator value is to 1, the stronger the relationship.
	Relationship directionality (impact) Larger path coefficients are shown as wider arrows and blue and red colors denote positive and negative effects, respectively. In cases where there is no directional impact relationship between the variables, it means that the variables are independent of the other variables in the model.
Weight (w)	The weight is shown in the model next to the corresponding arrow and indicates the relative contribution of the indicator to the corresponding latent variable. The values of this indicator range from 0 to 1 and implies that the closer the value of the indicator is to 1, the larger the contribution.

Table 2.
Outcome interpretation in PLS-PM models (multivariate analysis).

prosperity and development of logistics companies. The fulfillment of this objective is accomplished through the method:

Analysis of types of refusals and their consequences - Failure mode and effects analysis (FMEA). The method is defined and standardized by experts. After the expert team that has the necessary experience and knowledge of the object under study has been assembled, the methodology identifies and ranks the logistics risks under study. Irrespective of the ranking method, it is necessary to identify each logistics risk-specific program and actions to eliminate or minimize the negative impact.

The method applies to various fields of knowledge [3] but it is not known to have been applied to analyze the risks of nonconforming processes related to satisfaction in logistics services. This made it necessary to develop and apply a new methodology to assess nonconforming processes in logistics services, as one of the tasks for this chapter. The chapter investigates the risk in logistics processes that may contribute to the deterioration of satisfaction indicators in logistics services related to FMCG and, specifically, the food sector.

2.1 Assumptions and limitations in the risk analysis of noncompliant processes in logistics services

The methodology is essentially based on the following model assumptions:

- Detecting nonconforming logistics processes at a late-stage leads to higher costs for the company.

- The strategy of detecting and correcting nonconforming logistics processes can be replaced by the strategy to avoid them and eliminate the causes in the planning phase.
- The costs of controlling and tracking nonconforming logistics processes in the stages immediately preceding the physical delivery of goods can be minimized.
- The experience gained from noncompliant logistics processes can be used to address the cause of their reoccurrence in the future.
- The principle of error prevention should be prioritized in managing nonconforming logistics processes.
- Quality control of logistics services should be assigned to highly competent employees who play a role in the actual execution of the processes.

Limitations in the application of the method are related to the control over its management and can be defined in three main directions:

- The control of the risk of noncompliant logistics services is specific to each market segment and may impair its objectivity.
- Despite the measures to control the risks and to neutralize the negative impact of some factors, the developed methodology cannot completely eliminate the impact of all random factors.
- Although the analysis is based on real risks, the achievement of the residual risk values, after the implementation of the control measures, may not be fully consistent with the actual outcome given the influence of unknown factors in the assessment.
- Control measures need to be implemented for fully measurable outcomes of noncompliant logistics processes and those that cannot be measured with complete accuracy.
- The proposed control measures to manage the risks must be adapted to extreme changes in the external and internal environment.
- In establishing the Risk Priority Number (RPN) and its three components of Severity (S), Likelihood (O), and Detection (D), the assessment of the degree of risk assigned by the experts conducting the analysis can be highly subjective.
- The analysis based on expert opinion must also assess whether the three parameters are equally important. In cases where the experts judge that this is not the case, significance coefficients should be assigned to each of the components (S), (O), and (D).
- It should be considered that each factor requires different preventive actions to prevent or minimize the risk of a negative impact of the error or noncompliance occurring even in cases where the analysis results in identical RPN scores for different factors.

2.2 Assigning scores and interpreting results in the risk analysis of noncompliant processes in logistics services

To apply the method, a separate RPN (Risk Priority Number) must be determined for each process.

The numerical value of the RPN denoted the quantification of the risk that caused the nonconformity in the logistics service obtained as the product of the probability of the nonconformity occurring, the probability of the nonconformity being detected before the customers, and the severity of the impact in case it is not detected. The values for each of the RPN components can range from 1 to 10 as indicated in **Table 3**, determination of RPN risk class **Table 4**.

(S) Severity of consequences	(O) Probability of occurrence	(D) Probability of detection
8–10 A small change in the risk factor can make a significant difference in satisfaction with logistics services.	8–10 The risk factor is expected to have a negative impact on satisfaction	7–10 The possibility of detecting noncompliance before it affects satisfaction is negligible
5–7 A small change in the risk factor has the potential to significantly affect satisfaction with logistics services.	5–7 Significant likelihood that the risk factor will negatively impact satisfaction	4–6 There is little possibility of detecting noncompliance before it affects satisfaction
2–4 Changes in the risk factor have only a marginal impact on satisfaction with logistics services.	2–4 Risk factors unlikely to negatively impact satisfaction	2–3 The opportunity to identify noncompliance before it affects satisfaction is significant
1 Changes in the risk factor do not affect satisfaction with logistics services.	1 Negligible likelihood that the risk factor will negatively impact satisfaction	1 The discrepancy can be detected before it affects satisfaction

Table 3.
Determination of RPN components.

Value of RPN	Explanatory notes
RPN over 851 Very high-risk	The potential consequences of noncompliance can cause dissatisfaction, increase the churn of current and potential customers, and significantly degrade the performance metrics of the logistics services that are important to the customer.
RPN 600–850 High risk	The potential consequences of noncompliance can significantly degrade the satisfaction and performance metrics of logistics services that are important to the customer.
RPN 150 to 599 Moderate risk	The potential risk of noncompliance is likely to negatively impact satisfaction and degrade performance metrics for logistics services that are important to the customer to a moderate degree.
RPN up to 149 Low risk	A low-risk class is defined when the potential consequences of noncompliance will result in a temporary reduction in satisfaction.
RPN up to 10 Negligible risk	A negligible class is defined when the potential consequences of the noncompliance occurring will have no impact on the company's operations and customer satisfaction.

Table 4.
Determination of RPN risk class.

2.3 Setting of the empirical study for risk analysis

A pilot study was first brainstormed and conducted to test the feasibility of applying the FMEA method to analyze the risk of noncompliant logistics services related to customer satisfaction from 1 May 2020 to 15 May 2021. The pilot study was conducted with five leading logistics professionals and its results showed that all participants support the application of the FMEA method for analyzing logistics processes. Each participant in the pilot study was required to be an employed logistics manager with at least five years of experience in the field and demonstrated competence through the submission of diplomas and certificates.

The baseline survey was conducted through discussion and brainstorming from 01 June 2021 to 01 September 2021. A total of nine team meetings were held to assess the risk of noncompliant logistics processes using the FMEA method. The analysis team included 10 participants and one moderator. Each participant satisfied the criteria as an employed logistics manager (logistics as part of a manufacturing site or logistics services as an independent company) and had proven competence through the presentation of diplomas and certificates. The moderator took notes on the discussion based on which the main highlights of the participants' opinions were extracted.

2.4 Setting the empirical study to discuss and reach a consensus on risk analysis of noncompliant processes

The consensus was reached in the team meetings by following the steps outlined in **Figure 2**.

2.5 Setting the empirical study for risk analysis of noncompliant processes in logistics services

The method was used, based on the results obtained from the survey on customer satisfaction using the SERVQUA method conducted in the period from 15 February 2021 to 15 April 2021, to analyze possible inconsistencies and errors in the implementation of logistics processes and identify their causes and consequences. Within the framework of quality management in logistics, FMEA has been applied to enhance customer satisfaction and reliability of logistics services to prevent their nonconformance.

Potential system deficiencies are evaluated based on their significance to the customer, the likelihood of their occurrence, and the ability to detect and correct the nonconformity before losses or consequences are incurred. The method can be used to analyze not only planned but also actual processes where the risk of changes and the impact of these changes on the management of logistics activities must be assessed.

The essential advantages of the method are related to uncovering opportunities and adopting a quality management approach through risk management. The method implies performing analyses that enable a collaborative management approach within the logistics organization. In this way, quality management can be oriented towards the risks generated by dynamic changes in the external and internal environment, which are often the root cause of nonconformities in the system. Essential priorities of quality management in logistics should be the realization that quality deficits increase losses and the corporate philosophy must be changed to bring the quality management system back under the control of the logistics organization. The goal is to understand and accept that impeccable service can only be achieved through sustainable

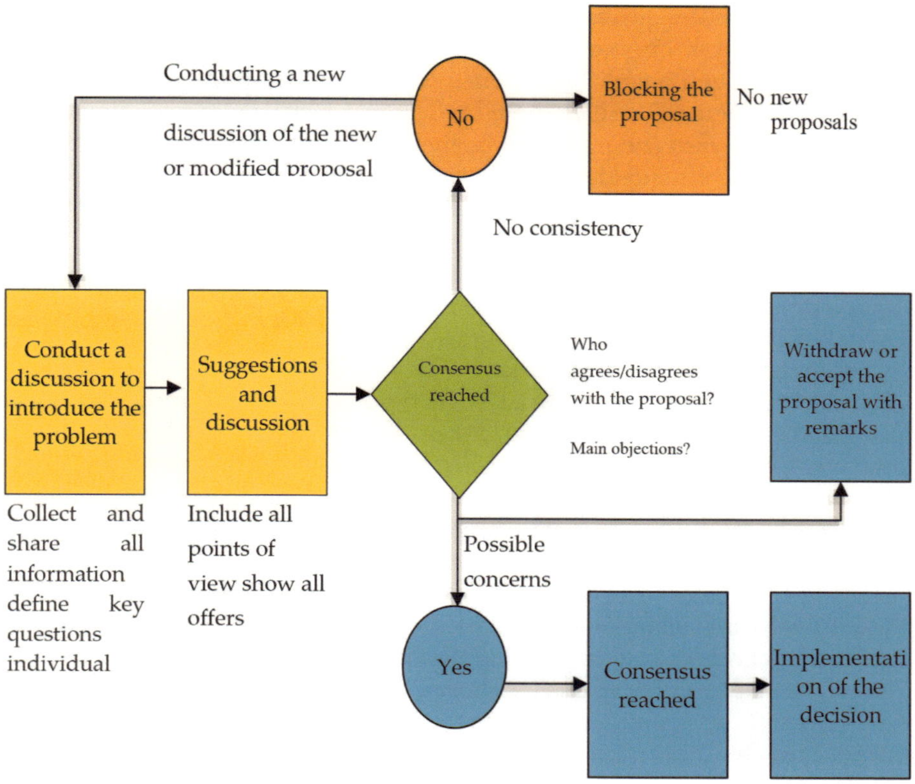

Figure 2.
Consensus model for risk analysis of noncompliant processes in logistics services.

compliance and improvement. The purpose of risk analysis is to identify and promptly address gaps in the service delivery system that negatively impact customer satisfaction.

The FMEA determines the likelihood of these gaps occurring and their potential consequences by assessing, in terms of severity, the measures required to prevent the risk, their effectiveness in specific situations, and the residual risk in the event of system failures. In cases where the method is adopted as a corporate philosophy in decision-making for new service offerings, risks of compromised quality should be identified and mitigated in accordance with the principles for applying the method.

2.6 Methodology for the analysis and summary of the results of the study on the risk of noncompliant processes in logistics services

The methodology to analyze and summarize the results of the study conducted on the risk of nonconforming processes is based on the Pareto analysis. The tool is named in honor of the Italian economist Pareto, who is also its creator [4]. In 1897, after annually analyzing the distribution of wealth in Italy, Pareto found that the incomes in the public were unequally distributed [5, 6]. The Pareto principle, also known as the 80/20 rule, states [7] that, for many events, approximately 20% of the causes contributing to 80% of the effect [8]; therefore, which are unequally distributed. The method can be applied after the significant causes of inconsistencies in the system are identified and analyzed, and losses will be minimized by eliminating them.

The method classifies quality problems in logistics services into two areas – few but essential and numerous but minor problems. This and other methods in quality management must be based on reliable information gathered from specific logistics services applied in practice. The data should reflect real events from economic processes that need to be analyzed and processed further. The analysis appropriately targets problem-solving efforts and identifies the main drivers of nonconformities. Juran interprets this principle by establishing that 20% of the causes of product defects create 80% of product problems.

The Pareto analysis was conducted simultaneously with the risk assessment of noncompliant logistics processes using the FMEA method and the same sample. The obtained data on the ex-ante and residual risk identified by the FMEA method were compared in the Pareto analysis procedure.

The values for upfront and residual risk from noncompliant logistics processes were tabulated in the procedure and the team assigned a percentage to each value such that the total was 100%. The percentages assigned were then used to construct a bar chart.

The Pareto analysis identified the differences in the ranking of causes before and after the implementation of corrective actions to the noncompliant logistics processes. The resulting diagrams have practical implications and can be used by senior management of logistics firms to prioritize actions and minimize risk.

XLSTAT software, which is embedded in Microsoft Excel's XLSTAT statistical analysis package, was used in conducting the Pareto analysis.

The following N number of qualitative or quantitative values were awarded in the Pareto analysis of the sample identified in the FMEA risk assessment of noncompliant logistics processes:

- Number of observations: The number N of values in the selected sample.
- Number of missing values: The number of missing values in the sample that are ignored in subsequent statistical calculations of the values.
- Sum of weights (Sw): The sum of the weights awarded, considering that all weights are equal to 1, Sw = n.
- Mode: The mode of the sample analyzed is the most common category.
- Mode frequency: The frequency of the category to which the mode corresponds.
- Category: The names of the different categories present in the sample.
- Relative frequency by category: The relative frequency of each category.
- Cumulative relative frequency by category: The cumulative relative frequency of each category.

Methods are also applied to analyze, systematize and differentiate various requirements that form satisfaction and help manage the quality of logistics services.

All the principles and methods of building management systems and the comparative analysis between different objects are also applied in the study. In addition to the listed main methods, the principles of quality and risk management required by the international standard ISO 9000:2015 and ISO 31000 have been applied.

The methods used in the chapter have the potential to help achieve its main objective and define the chapter design and the methods of data collection and analysis.

3. Conclusion

Due to the increasing market competition, a necessary condition for increasing customer satisfaction is the provision of qualified services that help organize timely deliveries of the goods requested by the customer. Through process controls, these processes could help to prevent nonconforming services from occurring prior to customer requirements.

The chapter of the study describes the conceptual framework of two groups of methods 1. Methodology for conducting the SERVQUA Satisfaction Analysis Survey (CAP) in Logistics and 2. Methodology for conducting the risk analysis study of noncompliant processes in logistics services. All the principles and methods of building management systems and the comparative analysis between different objects are also applied in the chapter. In addition to the listed main methods, the principles of quality and risk management required by the international standard ISO 9000: 2015 and ISO 31000 have been applied. The methods used in the chapter have the potential to help achieve its main objective and define the study design and the methods of data collection and analysis.

Author details

Marieta Stefanova
Department Management and Logistics, Nikola Vaptsarov Naval Academy, Varna, Bulgaria

*Address all correspondence to: m.stefanova@nvna.eu

References

[1] Tenenhaus M, Vinzi V, Chatelin Y, Lauro C. PLS path modeling. Computational Statistics & Data Analysis. 2005;**48**:159-205. DOI: 10.1016/j.csda.2004.03.005

[2] Addinsoft. XLSTAT 2021.3.1 Data Analysis and Statistics Software for Microsoft Excel. Paris, France: Addinsoft; 2021

[3] Satrisno A, Moo H, Lee T, Hyon J. Improvement strategy selection in FMEA: Classification, review and new opportunity roadmaps. Operat Suppl Ch Manag. 2013;**6**:54-63

[4] Alkiayat M. A Practical Guide to Creating a Pareto Chart as a Quality Improvement Tool. Global Journal on Quality and Safety in Healthcare. 2021;**4**: 83-84. DOI: 10.36401/JQSH-21-X1

[5] Pareto V, Lopreato J, Pareto V. Academic Dictionaries and Encyclopedias. New York: TY Crowell; 1965

[6] Mandelbrot BB, Hudson RL. The (mis) behaviour of markets: a fractal view of risk, ruin and reward. Second ed. London: Profile Books; 2010

[7] Wood J, McLure M. From Ethical to Economic Liberalism-the Sociology of Vilfredo Pareto: Critical Assessments of Leading Economists. Vilfredo Pareto: critical assessments of leading economists. London, New York: Taylor & Francis; 1999. pp. 430-455

[8] Cirillo R. Was Vilfredo Pareto Really a 'Precursor'of Fascism.? American Journal of Economics and Sociology. 1983;**42**:235-246. DOI: 10.1111/ j.1536-7150.1983.tb01708.x

Chapter 3

Logistics Services Satisfaction Survey: SERVQUA

Marieta Stefanova

Abstract

The chapter of the study presents the performed analysis of the logistics services satisfaction survey. It has been found that later the non-conformities in the logistics quality management system are identified and corrected, the more serious they are. The analysis is performed using the PLS-PM model captures the causal relationships of the study sample through arrows that start at a latent variable (factor) and point to the measured indicator variables. Results show that expected quality is the most important and effective latent variable. Customers were positive about the satisfaction of their requirements and the ability of logistics service providers to assess their expectations.

Keywords: logistics services satisfaction, PLS-PM

1. Introduction

> *Physical distribution is today's frontier in business. It is the one area where managerial results of great magnitude can be achieved. And it is still a largely unexplored territory'*
> *Peter Drucker* [1].

The later non-conformities in the logistics quality management system are identified and corrected, the more serious they are. Some of the non-conformities in the system may not be detected at all due to the complex requirements for completing and submitting information to the service provider or the control bodies that carry out counter-checks on the case:

- Process management requires addressing the root causes of non-conformances to minimise their recurrence [2–5].

- Significant cost reductions in quality management can be achieved if the system is planned appropriately for the conditions [6] and actual execution of the processes, rather than devoting additional costs to controlling inconsistencies and errors that would occur during the execution of the logistics processes.

- Quality and risk management are part of every business process [7–10]; only the application of expert opinions and methods is not applicable in day-to-day operations.

- The later the risk or non-compliance is discovered, the more difficult it will be to take adequate corrective action and the greater the cost of doing so.
- It is much more effective to address the causes of potential system failures at the process design stage than to look for methods to detect and correct inconsistencies.
- Applying the principle of good system planning to prevent errors is fundamental and leads to a reduction in overall costs.

The recipient of logistics services, who is a party to the supply contract, may bring an action against the supplier for breach of any expressed or implied term of the supply contract in relation to a non-conforming service. The supplier is obligated to take all reasonable steps to prevent acts or omissions which are reasonably foreseeable and expected to cause material damage. Any action taken to address operational risks shall be proportionate to the potential impact on the compliance of the logistics services [11].

Results of the satisfaction analysis in logistics services.

2. Analysis model of satisfaction

REBUS-PLS (a response-based procedure for detecting single segments in partial least squares modelling) was developed within the PLS-PM approach by Esposito Vinzi [12]. Many studies detect distinct behavioural differences that are caused naturally by the interactions that take place between the environment and its preferences. The analysis found that such differences often exist in the group studied and the differences clearly define two clusters of behaviour patterns.

The analysis was performed in Excel using the statistical software XLSTAT 2021.4.1.1201 – REBUS [13]. The number of classes was automatically determined during the cluster analysis with a chosen threshold of 95%. Three consecutive clustering operations were established, which created a binary cluster tree (dendrogram) with the root class containing all observations. The results are presented in **Figure 1**.

In the figure, it can be clearly observed that the first group (right) is more homogeneous than the second (it flatter on the dendrogram). This is confirmed when examining the within-class variance, which is much higher for the second group than for the first. In class 1, satisfaction is mainly explained by the perceived quality and in class 2, satisfaction is also explained by perceived quality but logistics service expectations have a less significant effect.

2.1 Agglomerative hierarchical clustering

REBUS algorithm: Dissimilarity: CM Index. Stop conditions: Iterations = 100 Threshold = 95%. The REBUS algorithm did converge after 99 iterations.

2.2 Analysis for the PLS-PM model of satisfaction

The PLS-PM model (estimated with XLSTAT 2021.4.1.1201-PLS-PM) captures the causal relationships of the study sample through arrows that start at a latent variable

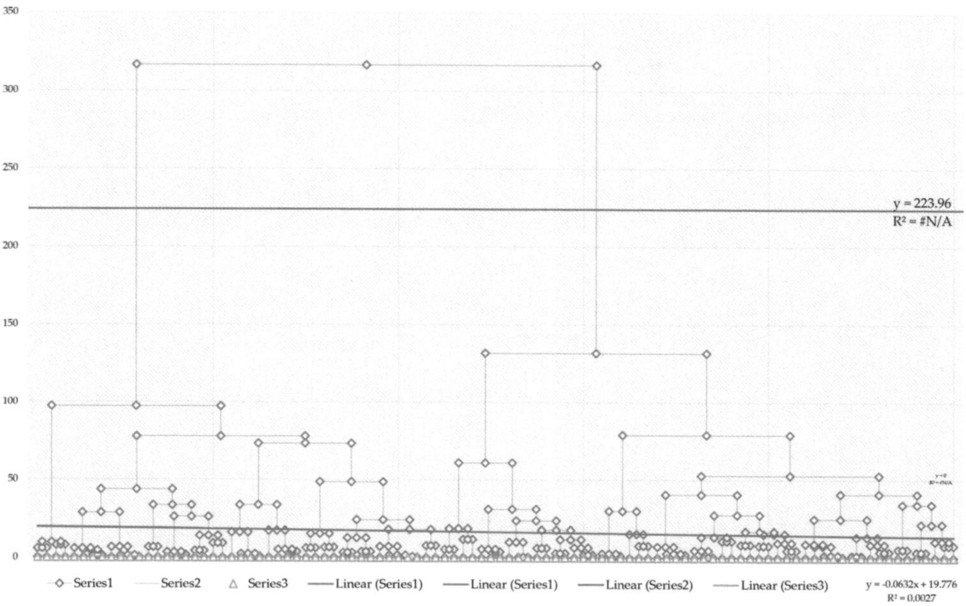

Figure 1.
Agglomerative hierarchical clustering (AHC). REBUS-PLS (response-based single segment detection procedure in partial least squares modelling).

(factor) and point to the measured indicator variables. The model specification (measurement model) is presented in **Table 1**.

The latent variables assessed in the model are Expectation: customer expectations related to logistics service culture; Quality: the expected quality of logistics services; Value: the perceived value of logistics services; Image: the reputation and tangible indicators of logistics services; Satisfaction: satisfaction derived from the comparison between the expected and actual perception of the logistics service; Complaints: customer complaints arising in the course of logistics service provision, unmet expectations, perceived or actual customer requirements, Loyalty: loyalty is the positive attitude of the customer towards the service provided. The type of model with latent variables is presented in **Figures 2** and **3**.

When running the model, the following criteria were set: Display: Expert and Marketing, Method: PLSPM, Stopping Conditions: Iterations = 5 /Convergence = 0.0001,

Latent variable Latent variable	**Image**	**Expectation**	**Perceived quality**	**Perceived value**	**Satisfaction**	**Complaints**	**Loyalty**
Number of manifested variables	5	2	5	2	3	2	2
Model	Model A	Model A	Model A	Model A	Model A	Model A	Model A
Type	Endogenous	Endogenous	Endogenous	Endogenous	Endogenous	Endogenous	Endogenous
Deflation	External	External	External	External	External	External	External

Table 1.
Model specification (measurement model).

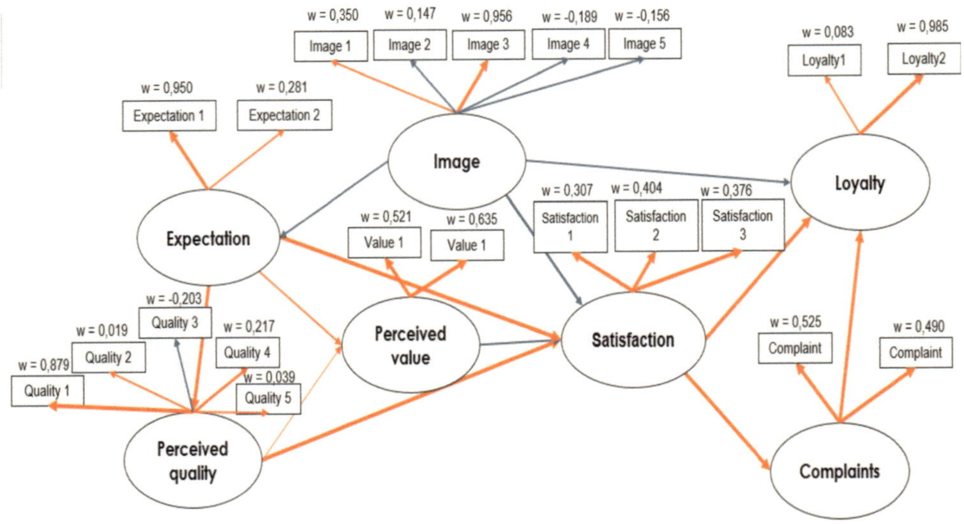

Figure 2.
Measurement model with manifested variables.

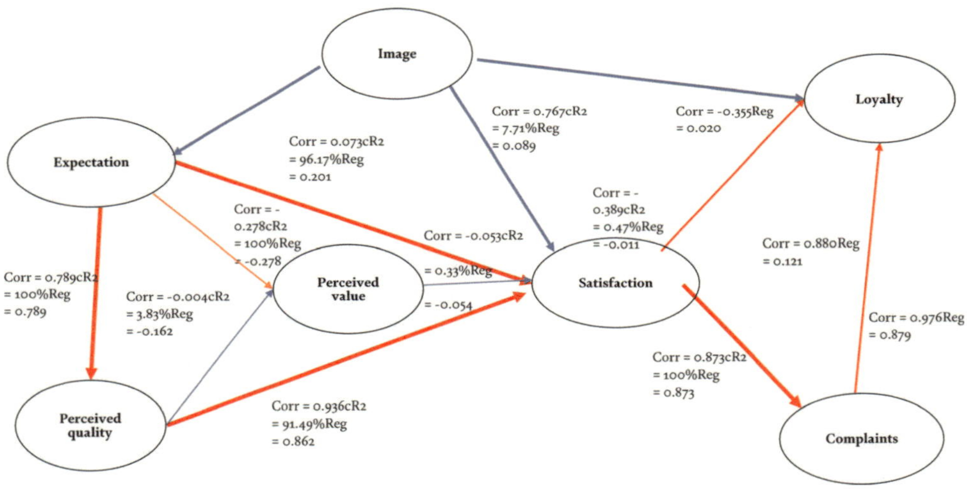

Figure 3.
Measurement model with values for Corr, R2, Reg.

Confidence Intervals: 95/Bootstrap /Resamplings = 100, Latent Variable Scores: Scale MV, Treatment of manifest variables: Standardised, weights on standardised MV, Values of the first eigenvector, Internal estimation: PLS, Score for latent variables: Standardised.

The first stage in the analysis is the confirmation of the reliability of the results obtained from the study based on the information collected about the data and the model created. The analysis is presented in **Table 2**.

Cronbach's alpha calculations in the following cases are below 0.7: expectancy, perceived value, and loyalty. For these latent variables, Dillon and Goldstein's rho is above 0.7 and the first eigenvalue is greater than the second. This leads us to

Latent variable	Dimensions	Cronbach's alpha	D.G. rho (PCA)	Condition number	Critical value	Eigenvalues
Customer expectations	2	0.068	0.782	1.036	1.000	1.035
						0.965
Perceived quality	5	0.760	0.855	1.484	1.000	1.544
						1.076
						0.924
						0.755
						0.701
Perceived value	2	0.660	0.855	1.715	1.000	1.493
						0.507
Satisfaction	3	0.905	0.941	3.888	1.000	2.522
						0.311
						0.167
Complaints from customers	2	0.969	0.985	5.650	1.000	1.939
						0.061
Loyalty	2	0.248	0.727	1.153	1.000	1.142
						0.858

Table 2.
Composite reliability variance of the outcome against the total variance (Monofactorial manifest variables).

believe that the data collected from the survey can be used for further analysis and interpretation.

A correlation matrix was constructed with the data, presented in **Table 3**.

The correlation analysis, presented in **Table 3**, shows the relationship between dependent and independent attributes.

According to Lorentz [14], correlation coefficients do not give a completely accurate picture of the extent to which a trait is a dependent trait in itself and through other traits. In his study, Lorentz proves that there is a limitation in the evaluation of correlation coefficients as these only show the magnitude and direction of the linear relationship between traits without revealing causal relationships. Thus, we performed further analyses based on path coefficients for latent variables.

The measurement model was found to be reliable and fit to the sample because the model fit indices were within the range recommended by Hu and Bentler [15].

3. Impact analysis and contribution of satisfaction variables

Once the measurement pattern has been studied, the structural model can be analysed. All the latent variables explored in the model are related to several other factors with several interpretable solutions. The results obtained for the latent variable satisfaction confirm its interrelationship with the other factors ($R^2 = 0.681$) (**Table 4**).

The first hypothesis aims to establish the relationship between satisfaction and perceived quality, expectancy, and image. Perceived quality (0.936) was found to have the strongest effect on satisfaction followed by customer expectations of logistics

6	Image 1	Image 2	Image 3	Image 4	Image 5	Expectation 1	Expectation 2	Quality 1	Quality 2	Quality 3	Quality 4	Quality 5	Value 1	Value 1	Satisfaction 1	Satisfaction 2	Satisfaction 3	Complaints 1	Complaints 2	Loyalty 1	Loyalty 2
Image 1	1.000	−0.113	−0.036	0.006	0.002	−0.063	−0.128	−0.131	−0.034	−0.084	−0.075	0.197	−0.095	−0.013	−0.115	−0.111	−0.176	−0.091	−0.081	0.093	−0.091
Image 2	−0.113	1.000	−0.146	0.178	0.008	−0.063	0.039	−0.104	0.055	0.090	−0.274	−0.119	0.073	−0.058	−0.107	−0.073	0.021	−0.037	0.009	0.051	−0.037
Image 3	−0.036	−0.146	1.000	0.044	0.053	−0.217	−0.139	−0.363	−0.105	0.039	0.169	0.051	0.099	0.225	−0.218	−0.326	−0.331	−0.321	−0.317	0.007	−0.321
Image 4	0.006	0.178	0.044	1.000	0.022	0.014	−0.093	0.095	0.202	−0.069	0.065	0.195	0.230	−0.043	0.071	0.100	0.088	0.101	0.096	−0.086	0.101
Image 5	0.002	0.008	0.053	0.022	1.000	0.055	0.038	0.050	−0.079	−0.067	0.091	0.028	0.024	−0.030	−0.038	0.063	0.017	0.056	0.099	0.073	0.056
Expectation 1	−0.063	−0.063	−0.217	0.014	0.055	1.000	0.035	0.806	−0.056	−0.015	0.143	−0.069	0.047	0.064	0.586	0.767	0.681	0.842	0.817	0.017	0.842
Expectation 2	−0.128	0.039	−0.139	−0.093	0.038	0.035	1.000	0.153	−0.113	−0.080	−0.027	−0.049	−0.110	0.124	0.070	0.192	0.295	0.152	0.099	0.226	0.152
Quality 1	−0.131	−0.104	−0.363	0.095	0.050	0.806	0.153	1.000	0.102	−0.112	0.162	0.032	−0.054	−0.034	0.764	0.965	0.860	0.944	0.891	0.109	0.944
Quality 2	−0.034	0.055	−0.105	0.202	−0.079	−0.056	−0.113	0.102	1.000	−0.098	−0.021	0.000	0.110	0.036	−0.010	0.115	−0.002	−0.002	0.043	0.117	−0.002
Quality 3	−0.084	0.090	0.039	−0.069	−0.067	−0.015	−0.080	−0.112	−0.098	1.000	−0.240	−0.220	−0.202	−0.128	−0.221	−0.136	−0.127	−0.089	−0.054	0.078	−0.089
Quality 4	−0.075	−0.274	0.169	0.065	0.091	0.143	−0.027	0.162	−0.021	−0.240	1.000	0.249	0.067	0.149	0.264	0.106	0.108	0.139	0.124	0.049	0.139
Quality 5	0.197	−0.119	0.051	0.195	0.028	−0.069	−0.049	0.032	0.000	−0.220	0.249	1.000	0.064	0.083	0.157	0.044	0.005	0.014	−0.007	0.092	0.014
Value 1	−0.095	0.073	0.099	0.230	0.024	0.047	−0.110	−0.054	0.110	−0.202	0.067	0.064	1.000	0.493	−0.017	−0.072	−0.157	−0.010	0.010	−0.079	−0.010
Value 1	−0.013	−0.058	0.225	−0.043	−0.030	0.064	0.124	−0.034	0.036	−0.128	0.149	0.083	0.493	1.000	0.061	−0.041	−0.056	0.003	0.016	−0.048	0.003
Satisfaction 1	−0.115	−0.107	−0.218	0.071	−0.038	0.586	0.070	0.764	−0.010	−0.221	0.264	0.157	−0.017	0.061	1.000	0.733	0.716	0.705	0.660	0.016	0.705
Satisfaction 2	−0.111	−0.073	−0.326	0.100	0.063	0.767	0.192	0.965	0.115	−0.136	0.106	0.044	−0.072	−0.041	0.733	1.000	0.832	0.907	0.853	0.097	0.907
Satisfaction 3	−0.176	0.021	−0.331	0.088	0.017	0.681	0.295	0.860	−0.002	−0.127	0.108	0.005	−0.157	−0.056	0.716	0.832	1.000	0.819	0.744	0.167	0.819
Complaints 1	−0.091	−0.037	−0.321	0.101	0.056	0.842	0.152	0.944	−0.002	−0.089	0.139	0.014	−0.010	0.003	0.705	0.907	0.819	1.000	0.939	0.142	1.000
Complaints 2	−0.081	0.009	−0.317	0.096	0.099	0.817	0.099	0.891	0.043	−0.054	0.124	−0.007	0.010	0.016	0.660	0.853	0.744	0.939	1.000	0.122	0.939
Loyalty 1	0.093	0.051	0.007	−0.086	0.073	0.017	0.226	0.109	0.117	0.078	0.049	0.092	−0.079	−0.048	0.016	0.097	0.167	0.142	0.122	1.000	0.142
Loyalty 2	−0.091	−0.037	−0.321	0.101	0.056	0.842	0.152	0.944	−0.002	−0.089	0.139	0.014	−0.010	0.003	0.705	0.907	0.819	1.000	0.939	0.142	1.000

Table 3.
Correlation matrix of the study.

Satisfaction	R^2	F	Pr > F		
	0.881	**176.635**	**0.000**		
Latent variable	Value	Standard error	T	Pr > |t|	f^2
Image	−0.011	0.039	−0.274	0.784	0.001
Expectations	0.089	0.058	1.527	0.130	0.025
Perceived quality	0.862	0.060	14.259	0.000	2.140
Perceived value	−0.054	0.036	−1.506	0.135	0.024

Table 4.
Path coefficients for the latent variable: Satisfaction.

services. The values obtained for the relationship between correlation and path coefficient support the hypothesis as perceived quality is 0.806, expectations are 0.068, perceived value is 0.003 and image is 0.004. Variable importance in the projection (VIP) was calculated, under VIPs (1 Comp / 5% conf. interval). The following chart (**Figure 4**) summarises the results obtained for the Impact and Contribution of Satisfaction Variables and their advisor VIPs in **Figure 5**.

The study made many assessments of the quality of each stage of customer service according to the most important criteria related to the image and tangibility of the services offered. It was found that customers evaluate the identified indicators of logistics task performance differently. In this study, the questions related to image variables 1, 2, and 3 have a positive relationship with satisfaction, while those related to image variables 4 and 5 have a negative relationship. Factor 4 was found to have the most significant influence on the overall satisfaction pattern and was related to the time between placing the request and receiving the delivery. The results obtained are presented in **Table 5**.

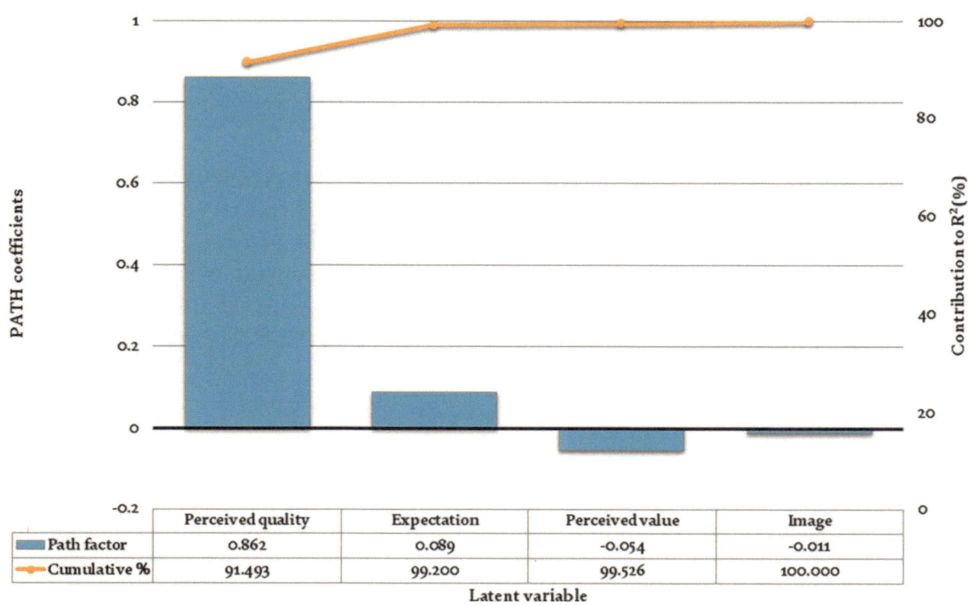

Figure 4.
Impact and contribution of satisfaction variables.

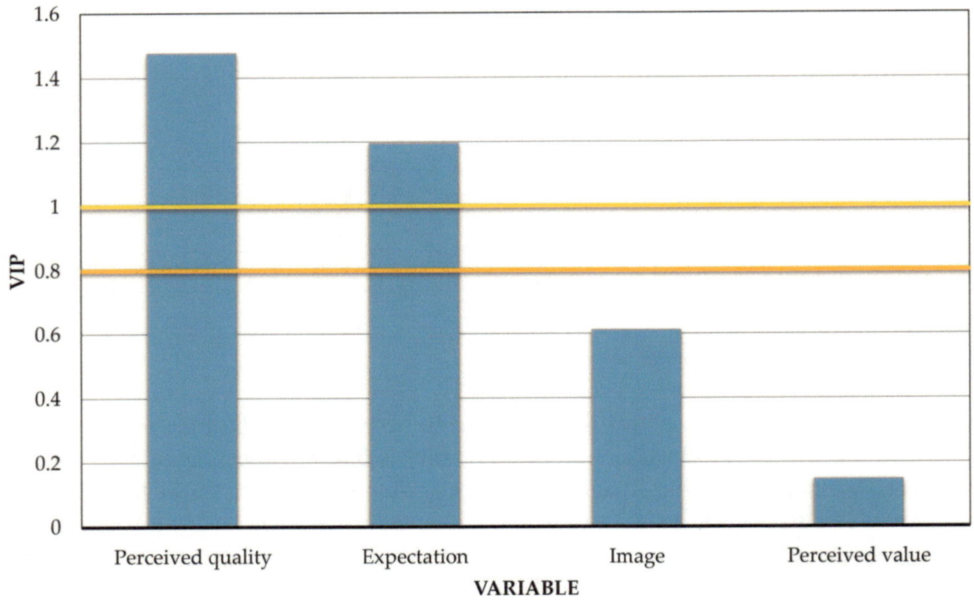

Figure 5.
Variable importance in the projection (1 comp / 5% conf. interval).

Latent variable	Variables of the manifest	External weight
Image	Image 1	0.344
	Image 2	0.146
	Image 3	0.956
	Image 4	−0.206
	Image 5	−0.150

Table 5.
Path coefficients for the latent variable: Image.

Customers of logistics services consider problem solving as one of their expectations of the logistics services provided. Expectations for logistics services are related to the knowledge and experience of the persons involved in the process and problems are solved operationally by the designated contact person. The image was found to have the most significant impact on expectations (0.077), the values obtained for the relationship between correlation and path coefficient are: 0.278 and are presented in **Table 6**.

Expectations	**R^2**	**F**	**Pr > F**		
	0.077	**8.230**	**0.005**		
Latent variable	Value	Standard error	t	Pr > |t|	f^2
Image	−0.278	0.097	−2.869	0.005	0.084

Table 6.
Path coefficients for the latent variable: Expectation.

The second hypothesis aims to establish the relationship between perceived quality and customer expectations. Expectations towards the logistics services provided also influence the overall satisfaction or service quality. The value obtained for the relationship between correlation and path coefficient is 0.789 and confirms the hypothesis at a p-value <0.05. The results are provided in more detail in **Table 7**. Therefore, this study proposes that companies that correctly perceive customer needs provide logistics services with better quality. To test the hypothesis, initial data from completed questionnaires were used, customers were asked to directly rate their service provider.

Customers relate their expectations of whether the logistics services meet their requirements (the specification) and whether these are reliable and on time to the perceived value of logistics services (the path coefficient is R^2 0.015). Meeting these requirements directly reduces the potential number of competitors and creates a significant competitive advantage (**Table 8**).

Customers who receive high-value services will also expect a high level of service. It can be assumed, based on the results obtained, that disappointment with the service quality is likely to encourage customers to seek alternative service providers, even though switching logistics providers will increase costs and cause time wastage. The results that confirm this hypothesis of impact and contribution of variables to the perceived value are presented in **Figure 6**.

The results also confirmed the hypothesis that there is a direct relationship between complaints and customer satisfaction with logistics services. Complaints were found to strongly impact satisfaction (path coefficient R^2 0.873). Providing quality services that meet the requirements without discrepancies or complaints will achieve greater customer confidence, minimise the risk of competition and ensure customer loyalty and increase the logistics provider's welfare from potential service revenue. The calculations of the significance coefficients (**Table 9**) show this hypothesis to be true.

Dynamic changes in the external environment deepen the drive for customer satisfaction, which is strongly influenced by the overall quality of logistics services. Satisfying customers' service quality requirements influence business performance and promote customer loyalty. Customer loyalty depends on a variety of factors, such as perceived service quality, personal preferences and expectations, social

Perceived quality	**R^2**	**F**	**Pr > F**		
	0.622	**161.543**	**0.000**		
Latent variable	Value	Standard error	t	Pr > |t|	f^2
Expectations	0.789	0.062	12.710	0.000	1.648

Table 7.
Path coefficients for the latent variable: Quality.

Perceived value	**R^2**	**F**	**Pr > F**		
	0.015	**0.755**	**0.473**		
Latent variable	Value	Standard error	t	Pr > |t|	f^2
Expectations	0.201	0.164	1.228	0.222	0.016
Perceived quality	−0.162	0.164	−0.991	0.324	0.010

Table 8.
Path coefficients for the latent variable: Perceived value.

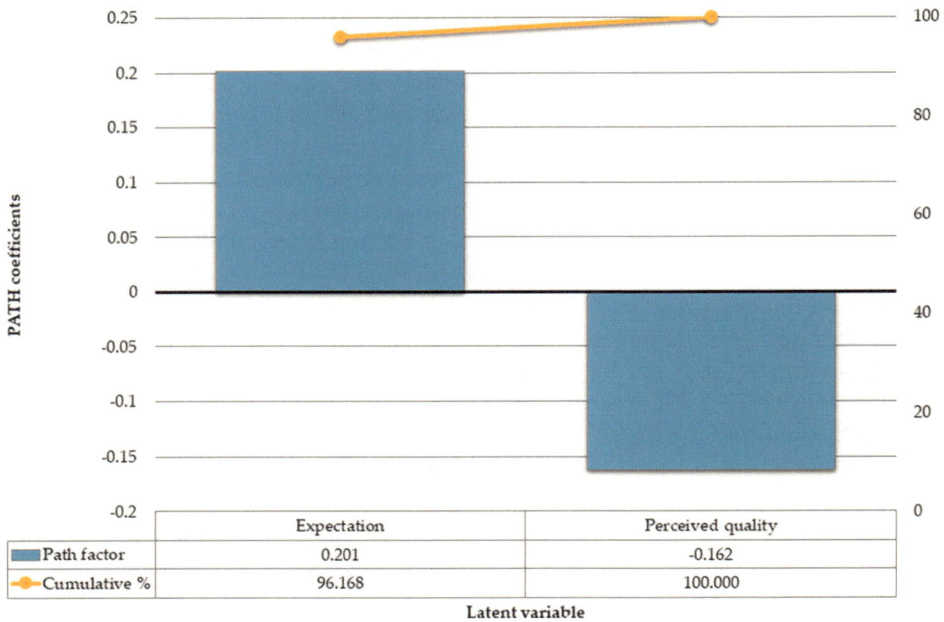

Figure 6.
Impact and contribution of variables: Perceived value.

Complaints	**R^2**	**F**	**Pr > F**		
	0.763	**314.882**	**0.000**		
Latent variable	Value	Standard error	t	Pr > |t|	f^2
Satisfaction	0.873	0.049	17.745	0.000	3.213

Table 9.
Path coefficients for the latent variable: Complaints.

Loyalty	**R^2**	**F**	**Pr > F**		
	0.957	**712.592**	**0.000**		
Latent variable	Value	Standard error	t	Pr > |t|	f^2
Image	0.020	0.023	0.878	0.382	0.008
Satisfaction	0.121	0.044	2.755	0.007	0.079
Complaints	0.879	0.044	20.170	0.000	4.238

Table 10.
Path coefficients for the latent variable: Loyalty.

interaction [16], customer experience in dealing with logistics providers, and many other specifically subjective factors. Furthermore, it is necessary to bear in mind that customer loyalty is not an objective assessment of the real situation but an emotional element. The hypothesis that loyalty strongly influences the satisfaction of customer expectations is confirmed by the results obtained for the path coefficient is R^2 0.957 (**Table 10**).

Customer loyalty is assessed as a consequence of the process and presented with recommendations for the logistics services used in the long and short term. The results confirming the impact hypothesis and the contribution of the loyalty variables are presented in **Figure 7**.

Marketing analyses of the survey data were also conducted to seek recommendations for customer satisfaction management. An IPMA (Importance performance matrix analysis) was performed and the visualised results are presented in **Figure 8**. This analysis is based on the importance and effectiveness of customer satisfaction and demonstrates the extent of the relationship between the exogenous and endogenous variables that can be derived. The partial least squares modelling method for structural equations with XLSTAT PLS is used to establish IPM

Results show that expected quality is the most important and effective latent variable. A high score was also found for customer expectations related to the logistics services provided. The fastest change in satisfaction can be achieved with the improvement of image impact and expected value. To explore this potential in more detail, incentive diagrams **Figures 9** and **10** were constructed. The values in **Figure 9** shows how the value of the target latent variable score would change if an improvement of x% is applied to the manifested variable. In the simulation results for the weight for predicting satisfaction (latent variable), the most important variables are perceived quality, expectations, perceived value, and image. The values in **Figure 10** show the manner in which the mean value of the target latent variable will change if an improvement of x% is applied to the manifested variable. In the simulation results for the weight for predicting satisfaction (latent variable), the most important manifestation variables are Quality 1, Expectation 1, Image 3, Expectation 2, Quality 4, Quality 3, Image 1, Image 4, Value 1, Image 5, Image 2, Value 1, Quality 2, and Quality 5.

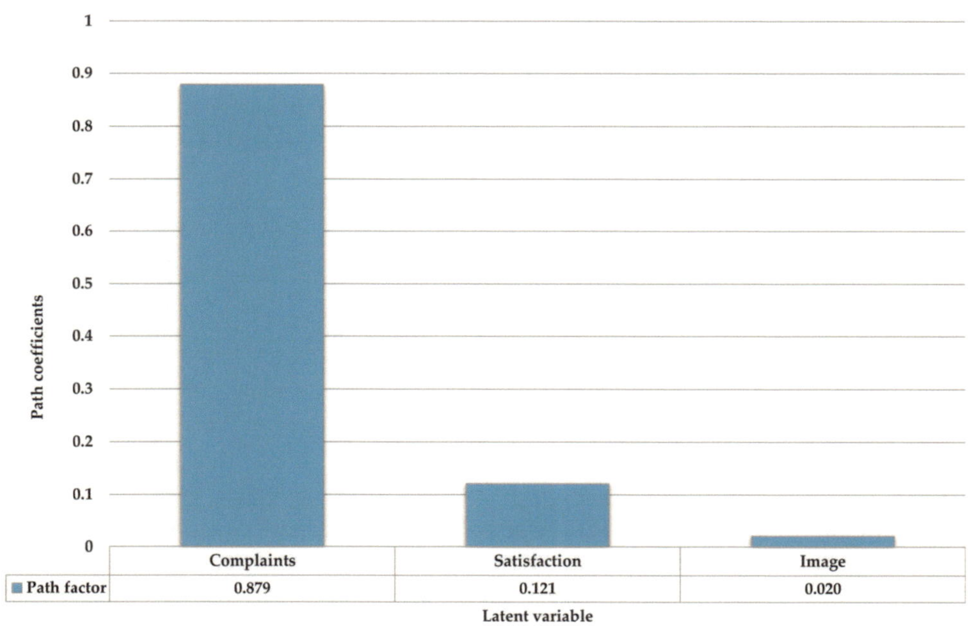

Figure 7.
*Impact and contribution of **loyalty** variables*

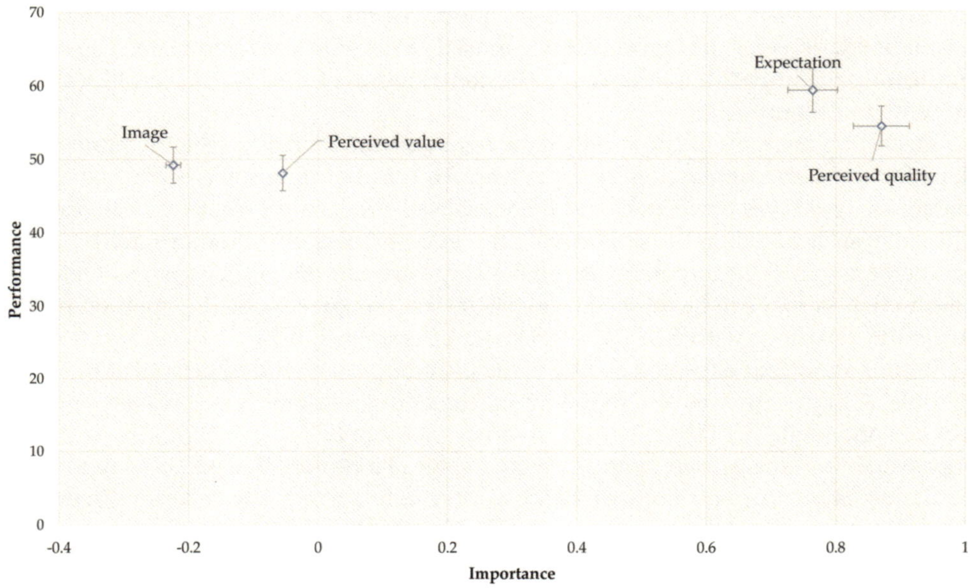

Figure 8.
Latent variables on a target variable (importance performance matrix analysis – IPMA).

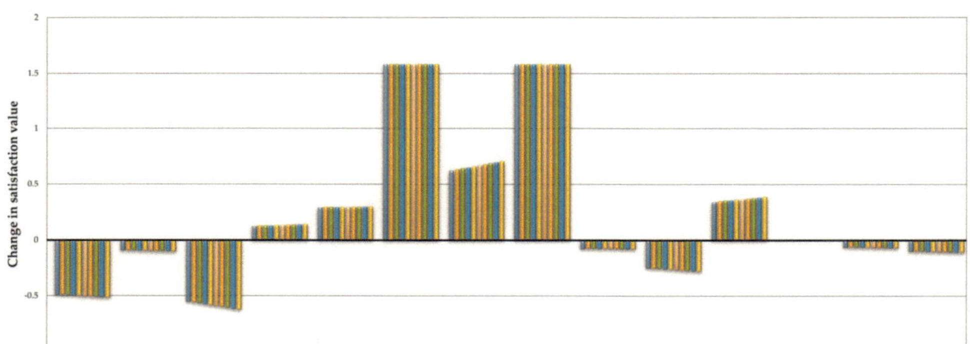

	Image 1->(Satisfaction)	Image 2->(Satisfaction)	Image 3->(Satisfaction)	Image 4->(Satisfaction)	Image 5->(Satisfaction)	Expectation 1->(Satisfaction)	Expectation 2->(Satisfaction)	Quality 1->(Satisfaction)	Quality 2->(Satisfaction)	Quality 3->(Satisfaction)	Quality 4->(Satisfaction)	Quality 5->(Satisfaction)	Value 1->(Satisfaction)	Value 1->(Satisfaction)
0	0.000	0.000	0.000	0.000	0.000	0.000	0.000	0.000	0.000	0.000	0.000	0.000	0.000	0.000
1	-0.491	-0.091	-0.554	0.121	0.287	1.584	0.624	1.584	-0.076	-0.249	0.339	0.005	-0.062	-0.098
2	-0.494	-0.092	-0.562	0.123	0.288	1.584	0.633	1.584	-0.076	-0.253	0.344	0.005	-0.063	-0.099
3	-0.498	-0.093	-0.571	0.125	0.289	1.584	0.642	1.584	-0.077	-0.256	0.349	0.005	-0.064	-0.101
4	-0.501	-0.095	-0.579	0.126	0.289	1.584	0.651	1.584	-0.077	-0.260	0.354	0.005	-0.065	-0.102
5	-0.504	-0.096	-0.587	0.128	0.290	1.584	0.661	1.584	-0.078	-0.264	0.359	0.005	-0.066	-0.103
6	-0.507	-0.097	-0.595	0.130	0.291	1.584	0.670	1.584	-0.078	-0.267	0.364	0.005	-0.067	-0.105
7	-0.511	-0.099	-0.603	0.132	0.292	1.584	0.679	1.584	-0.079	-0.271	0.369	0.005	-0.068	-0.106
8	-0.514	-0.100	-0.612	0.134	0.292	1.584	0.688	1.584	-0.079	-0.275	0.374	0.005	-0.069	-0.108
9	-0.517	-0.101	-0.620	0.135	0.293	1.584	0.697	1.584	-0.080	-0.278	0.379	0.005	-0.069	-0.109
10	-0.520	-0.103	-0.628	0.137	0.294	1.584	0.707	1.584	-0.080	-0.282	0.384	0.005	-0.070	-0.111

Variables of the manifest

Figure 9.
Incentive diagram of change in satisfaction value.

In summary of the analyses, it may be concluded that service providers who want to attract potential service users must first appropriately understand their expectations of service quality as it has a direct impact on customer satisfaction. High-quality logistics services increase service providers' advantages and customer loyalty. The study showed that customers prefer a company that provides quality services and takes steps to reduce complaints from customers.

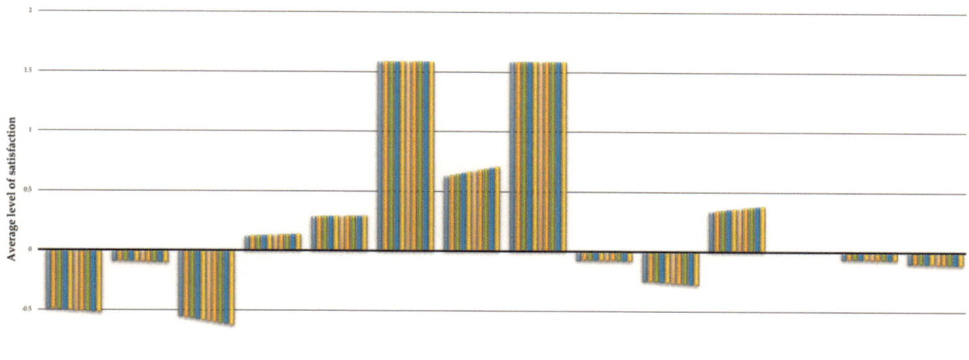

	Image 1->(Satisfaction)	Image 2->(Satisfaction)	Image 3->(Satisfaction)	Image 4->(Satisfaction)	Image 5->(Satisfaction)	Expectation 1->(Satisfaction)	Expectation 2->(Satisfaction)	Quality 1->(Satisfaction)	Quality 2->(Satisfaction)	Quality 3->(Satisfaction)	Quality 4->(Satisfaction)	Quality 5->(Satisfaction)	Value 1->(Satisfaction)	Value 1->(Satisfaction)
0	0.000	0.000	0.000	0.000	0.000	0.000	0.000	0.000	0.000	0.000	0.000	0.000	0.000	0.000
1	-0.491	-0.091	-0.554	0.121	0.287	1.584	0.624	1.584	-0.076	-0.249	0.339	0.005	-0.062	-0.098
2	-0.494	-0.092	-0.562	0.123	0.288	1.584	0.633	1.584	-0.076	-0.253	0.344	0.005	-0.063	-0.099
3	-0.498	-0.093	-0.571	0.125	0.289	1.584	0.642	1.584	-0.077	-0.256	0.349	0.005	-0.064	-0.101
4	-0.501	-0.095	-0.579	0.126	0.289	1.584	0.651	1.584	-0.077	-0.260	0.354	0.005	-0.065	-0.102
5	-0.504	-0.096	-0.587	0.128	0.290	1.584	0.661	1.584	-0.078	-0.264	0.359	0.005	-0.066	-0.103
6	-0.507	-0.097	-0.595	0.130	0.291	1.584	0.670	1.584	-0.078	-0.267	0.364	0.005	-0.067	-0.105
7	-0.511	-0.099	-0.603	0.132	0.292	1.584	0.679	1.584	-0.079	-0.271	0.369	0.005	-0.068	-0.106
8	-0.514	-0.100	-0.612	0.134	0.292	1.584	0.688	1.584	-0.079	-0.275	0.374	0.005	-0.069	-0.108
9	-0.517	-0.101	-0.620	0.135	0.293	1.584	0.697	1.584	-0.080	-0.278	0.379	0.005	-0.069	-0.109
10	-0.520	-0.103	-0.628	0.137	0.294	1.584	0.707	1.584	-0.080	-0.282	0.384	0.005	-0.070	-0.111

VARIABLES OF THE MANIFEST

Figure 10.
Incentive diagram for average level of satisfaction.

4. Conclusion

The study establishes that customers value not only the quality of service but also the expected value of the service provided, the good image of the logistics company is directly related to the competence of the staff who should be personally involved in solving the problems of risks arising from non-conforming supplies or processes.

The study shows that logistics service providers are aware and perceptive of customer expectations and can meet them, as the satisfaction indicators surveyed are more positive than negative. Customers were positive about the satisfaction of their requirements and the ability of logistics service providers to assess their expectations.

The study also proves that logistics firms need to manage the risks of non-compliant logistics services and minimise them, which will be discussed in the next chapter.

Acknowledgements

A huge thank you to my colleagues at the Department of Management and Logistics for encouraging this project.

I also thank all the logistics companies and users of logistics services who participated in the survey and shared their experiences.

I also thank the "N. Vaptsarov" Naval Academy for opening opportunities and providing access to world-class educational and scientific resources and assistance from distinguished professors with scientific interests in the field of my research.

Thank you to all the organisations that hired me as a consultant and helped me strive for lifelong learning.

Author details

Marieta Stefanova
Department of "Management and Logistics", Nikola Vaptsarov Naval Academy, Varna, Bulgaria

*Address all correspondence to: m.stefanova@nvna.eu

References

[1] Drucker P. The economy's dark continent. Fortune. 1962;**65**:265-270

[2] Ask C, Trygged M. Enhancing Problem Solving by Improving the Identification of Root Causes to Avoid Reoccurring Non-conformances. Gothenburg: Chalmers University of Technology; 2016

[3] Lee HL, Whang S. Higher supply chain security with lower cost: Lessons from total quality management. International Journal of Production Economics. 2005;**96**:289-300. DOI: 10.1016/j.ijpe.2003.06.003

[4] Prokopowicz D, Gołębiowska A. Business Intelligence Analytics Based on the Processing of Large Sets of Information with the Use of Sentiment Analysis and Big Data. Warsaw, Poland: Publishing House SGSP; 2021. pp. 129-154

[5] Zafirova T. Integration of the processes of strategic and crisis Management in the Conditions of crisis. Известия на Съюза на учените – Варна Серия Икономически науки. 2021;**10**: 158-168

[6] Lambert D, Douglas M, James R. Strategic Logistics Management. 4th ed. Homewood: McGraw-Hill Education; 1993

[7] Lai K, Vejvar M, Lun V. Risk in port logistics: Risk classification and mitigation framework. International Journal of Shipping and Transport Logistics. 2020;**12**:576-596

[8] Zafirova T. Impact of changes in the environment on the strategic aspects of crisis management. Izvestia Journal of the Union of Scientists – Varna Economic Sciences Series. 2021;**10**: 184-192

[9] Thai V. Logistics service quality: Conceptual model and empirical evidence. International Journal of Logistics Research and Applications. 2013;**16**:114-131. DOI: 10.1080/13675567.2013.804907

[10] Olson D, Wu D. Supply chain risk management. In: New Frontiers in Enterprise Risk Management. 1st ed. Berlin, Heidelberg: Springer; 2008

[11] Craighead CW, Blackhurst J, Rungtusanatham MJ, Handfield RB. The severity of supply chain disruptions: Design characteristics and mitigation capabilities. Decision Sciences. 2007;**38**: 131-156. DOI: 10.1111/j.1540-5915.2007.00151.x

[12] Evans M. Domesday marketing? From an inaugural lecture. Journal of Marketing Management. 1994;**10**: 409-431. DOI: 10.1080/0267257X.1994.9964287

[13] Addinsoft. XLSTAT 2021.3.1 Data Analysis and Statistics Software for Microsoft Excel. Paris, France: Addinsoft; 2021

[14] Lorentz L. Production and body composition traits of broilers in relation to breast weight evaluated by path analysis. Scientia Agricola. 2011;**68**: 320-325. DOI: 10.1590/S0103-90162011000300008

[15] Hu L, Bentler PM. Cutoff criteria for fit indexes in covariance structure analysis: Conventional criteria versus new alternatives. Structural Equation Modeling: A Multidisciplinary Journal. 1999;**6**:1-55. DOI: 10.1080/10705519909540118

[16] Kanev D. Commitment as a constraint to the pursuit of self-interest. Economics. 2017;**1**:3-20

Chapter 4

Investigation of the Risks of Non-Conforming Services in Logistics: Failure Mode and Effects Analysis (FMEA)

Marieta Stefanova

Abstract

After the analyses were performed using the SERVQUA model, the results were used for risk analysis (FMEA) to identify the causes, assessment, and consequences of logistics services that do not meet customer expectations. FMEA analysis was used as a method to investigate the consequences of emerging risks by quantifying the severity, likelihood of occurrence, and detection of non-conforming logistics services that further generated the RPN. Suggestions for specific actions to manage risks and opportunities that can be used for optimisation or improvement are also provided. From the analyses, it can be concluded that the main reasons for the decline in customer satisfaction are poorly managed logistics processes caused by the lack of sufficiently competent employees ready to deal with emerging risks and human errors.

Keywords: FMEA, logistics services, non-conformities, risk

1. Introduction

Although the need for risk management in logistics arises as an alternative to commercial insurance; a good practice is to adequately manage it as a form of contingency insurance in the normal practice of logistics organisations. Risk management is concerned with the development of a crisis management plan should an adverse event occur. Mikušová finds that senior management of smaller organisations is very sceptical about their ability to manage risks and consequently a crisis. Under a crisis, their solution is to dismiss employees and wait for more favourable conditions [1]. Most managers believe that preventing crises by planning specific actions in the event of an adverse event is costly and the benefits are not always proven [2–5]. Some studies have found that managers do not invest resources in crisis prevention because they believe that the crisis will, in most cases, unfold differently than their expectations [6, 7]. Other managers believe that there is no need to make such response plans [8] because their organisation is strong enough to overcome any risk and has the right strategic partner, the perfect product, or sufficient financial backing [9, 10]. A crisis resulting from dynamic changes in the external environment has the potential to threaten the sustainability and put the survival of the company at risk [11] if adequate action is not taken to overcome it [12]. The positive impact of the analysis of potential risks to the business is the ability to uncover the means of optimising it. It should be

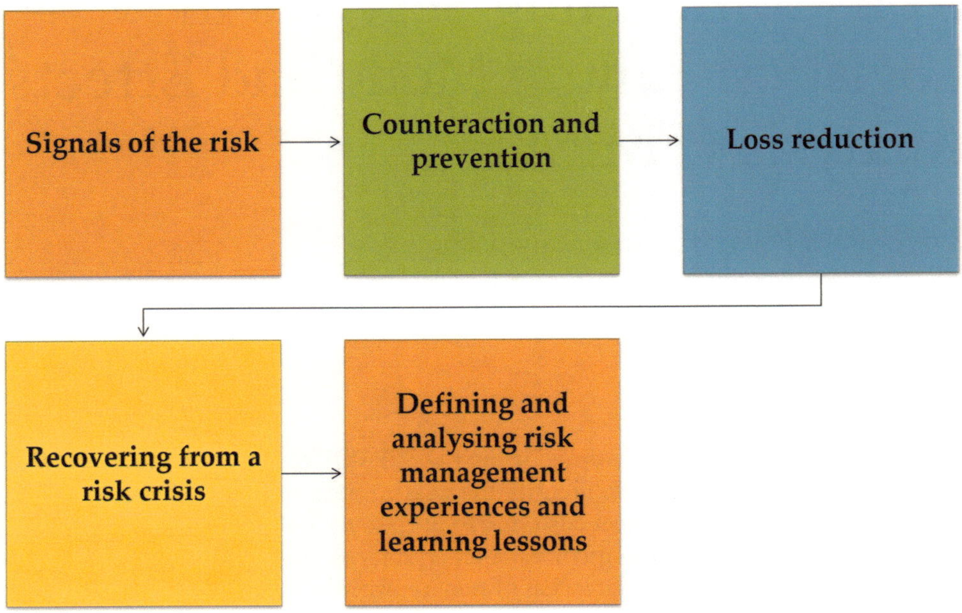

Figure 1.
Stages in crisis management (adapted from Pearson and Mitroff) [13].

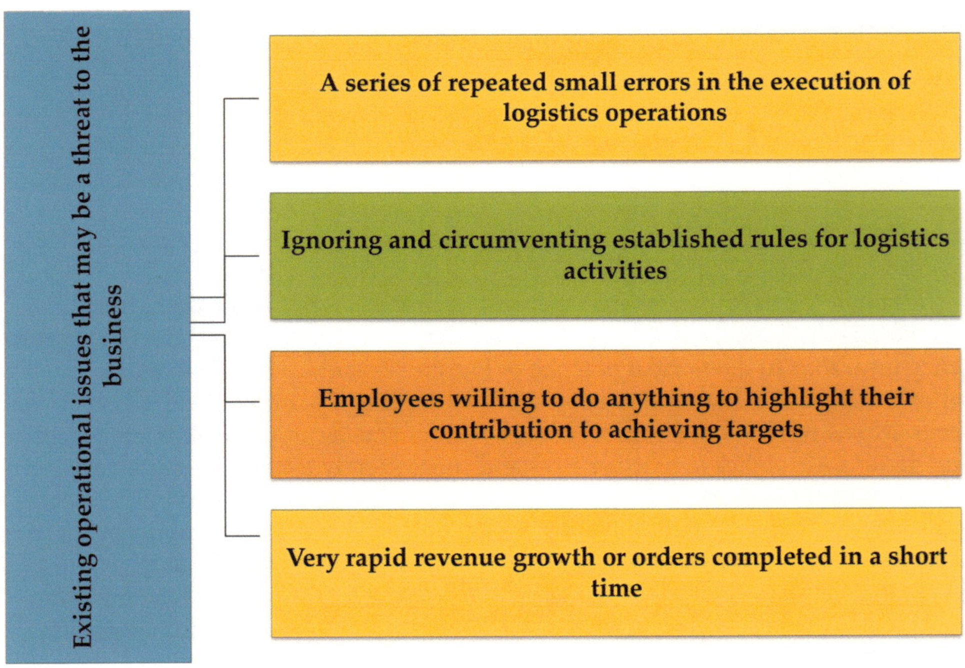

Figure 2.
Crisis warning signals (adapted from Pearson and Mitroff) [13].

noted that the causes of the same risk may be different—internal and external to the organisation. This study finds that most management crises start as small problems that are overlooked and ignored. In the longer term, these problems grow into crises that can deepen and threaten the reputation and survival of the business. To avoid this development, smouldering risks that have the potential to grow into a crisis for the business must be minimised. Several distinguishing features help to overcome and minimise risk in logistics, the most important of which is related to taking immediate measures that can jeopardise the performance of delivery contracts and unfortunately are not within the control of the logistics company. Pearson and Mitroff find that most crises go through several stages, as shown in **Figure 1** [13].

Several warning signs of major operational problems have been identified, which have the potential, in most cases, to escalate into a crisis for the business. These are presented in **Figure 2**.

2. Investigation of the risks of non-conforming services in logistics - failure mode and effects analysis (FMEA)

The risk analysis of non-compliant processes in logistics services using the FMEA analysis was conducted by the steps, shown in **Figure 3**:

2.1 Stage 1. Scoping

The main objective of scoping using FMEA analysis is to investigate the impact of risk factors that could affect the identified gaps between satisfaction and needs of customers or users of logistics services and that, as a consequence, negatively affect the financial performance of the FMCG logistics business. The results of the analysis can be used to prevent these factors from occurring or to reduce their impact and reach the required level of quality and efficiency.

The scope of the FMEA analysis includes the risk factors for the identified gaps between the satisfaction and needs of customers-users of logistics services, which directly or indirectly impact the prosperity of the organisation in the sample.

2.2 Stage 2. Define the constraints of the logistics processes and their corresponding inconsistencies

- The first set of constraints related to the application of qualitative analysis and whether there is a risk of non-compliance. Subsequently, only the identified risks are assessed, which implies that some risks are neglected.

- The second set of limitations relates to the timing of the analysis. For some risks, the estimate may be understated or overstated if the risk has a more significant short-term impact at that particular time.

2.3 Stage 3. Define and decompose the individual processes and sub-processes to be studied to obtain single components

Risk factors that can negatively affect customer satisfaction and needs can occur in any logistics service management process. Thus, we use FMEA analysis for the overall planning and management of processes related to logistics service quality

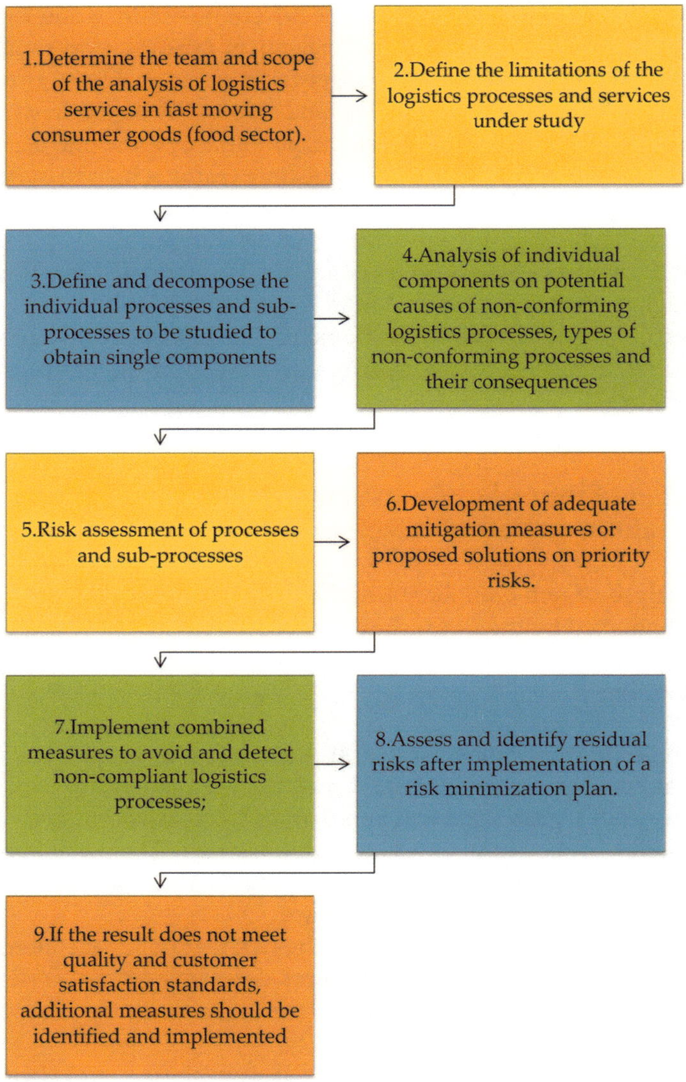

Figure 3.
Main stages of conducting FMEA in logistics services.

management. The processes for delivering customer satisfaction are divided into sub-processes and work operations. The steps of the overall process and the definition of the operations are summarised in a flowchart for greater visibility and accessibility during the analysis and are presented in **Figure 4**.

The relationships between the different units in logistics organisations are of primary importance to achieve the efficiency of any business. Within a logistics organisation, it is good practice to identify several centres of financial responsibility that aim to define the precise authority and responsibility of each unit and the strategic priorities to spend the incoming cash flows. Traditionally, four levels of financial responsibility are considered, as shown in **Figure 5**.

The financial responsibility for managing expenditure should rest with the department responsible for the entire range of services, which require the utilisation of the budget set by the higher-ups. Optimising the nomenclature of service offerings is,

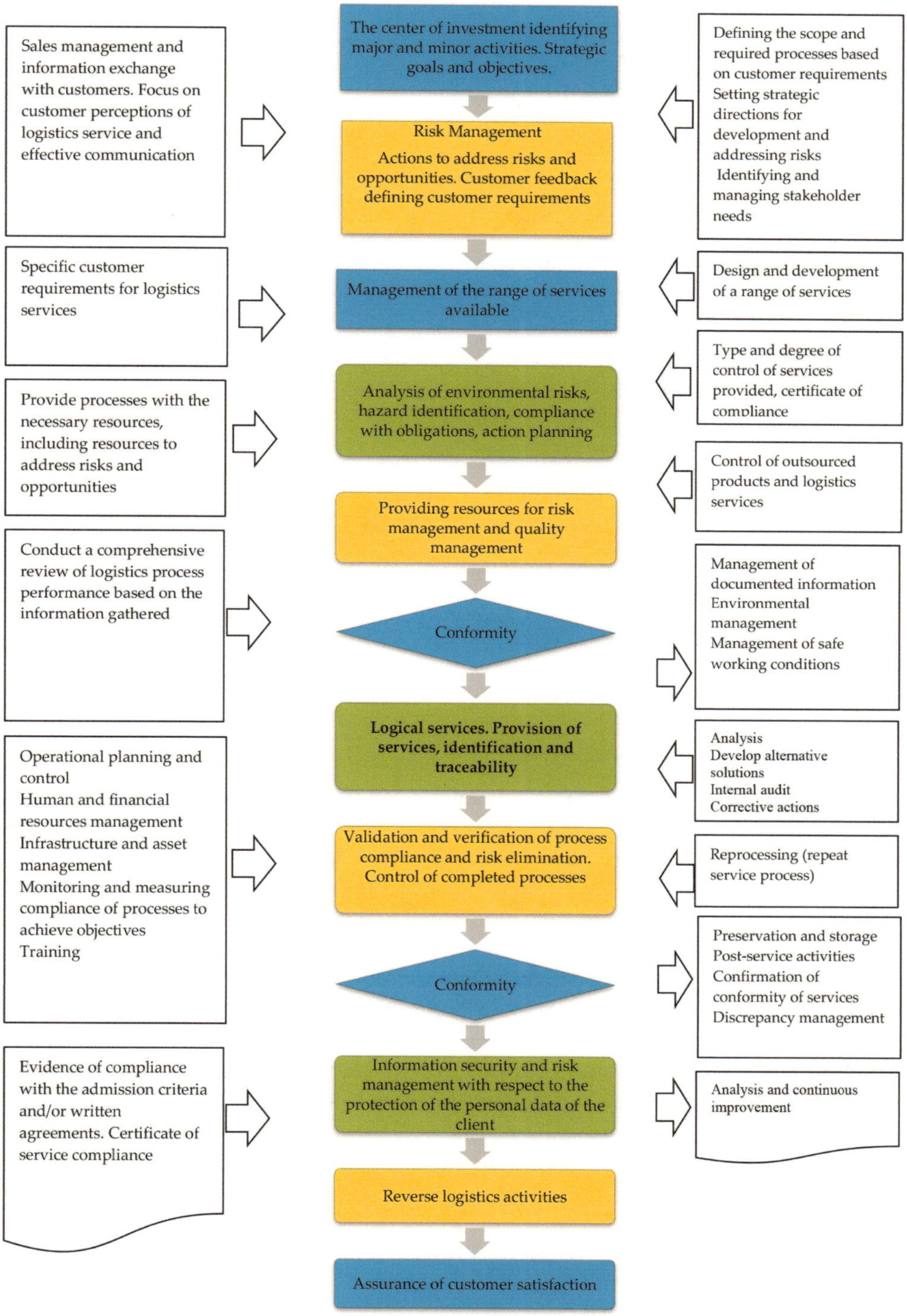

Figure 4.
Managing a compliant logistics service.

unfortunately, not in their remit, as at this level, they only implement strategic objectives. A very wide range or a rapid expansion of the logistics service portfolio is a common cause of financial insolvency for many organisations in the supply chain.

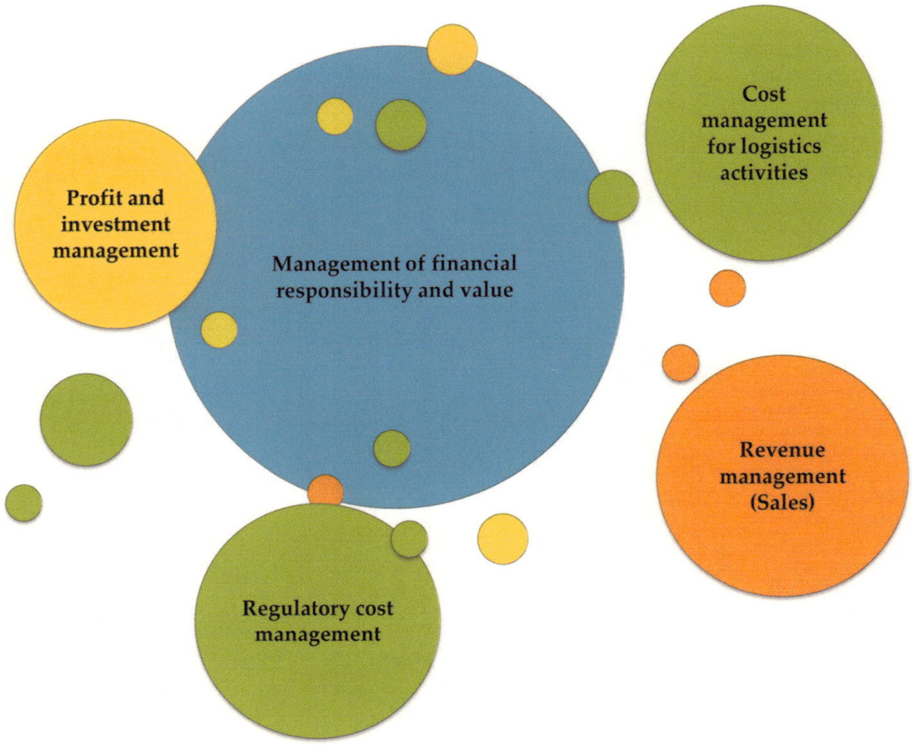

Figure 5.
Financial responsibility in logistics by department.

This is also the main reason for inconsistencies in sustainable service quality as too wide a range makes it difficult to control the activity and hinders specialisation in and improvement of the service delivery process. Management at this level is based on controlling deviations from pre-drawn higher-level budgets and the efficient use of working capital, which must be available to facilitate activity.

The financial responsibility for income management should rest with the department responsible for effective customer communication and providing the business with fresh funds to operate the organisation. Achieving compliance in the business is about building effective channels of communication and collecting receivables from customers based on sales volumes realised in value terms. The results of operations are related to the actual sales revenue collected, which is a significant contributor to the formation of profit or marginal income that is realised after deducting variable costs from the collections. In the context of quality management in logistics, this centre has the following priorities:

- Responsible for the development, implementation, and maintenance of the risk management framework.
- Presents and introduces the necessary actions to overcome risks and create opportunities.
- Undertakes specific activities to ensure organisational confidence that the logistics system can achieve intended results to improve desired trends and effects and prevent or reduce undesired trends and effects.

- Prepares information to analyse the effectiveness of actions addressing risks and opportunities and includes suggestions for improvement and risk treatment that require additional resources and (or) involve significant changes in the management of the logistics organisation's operations.

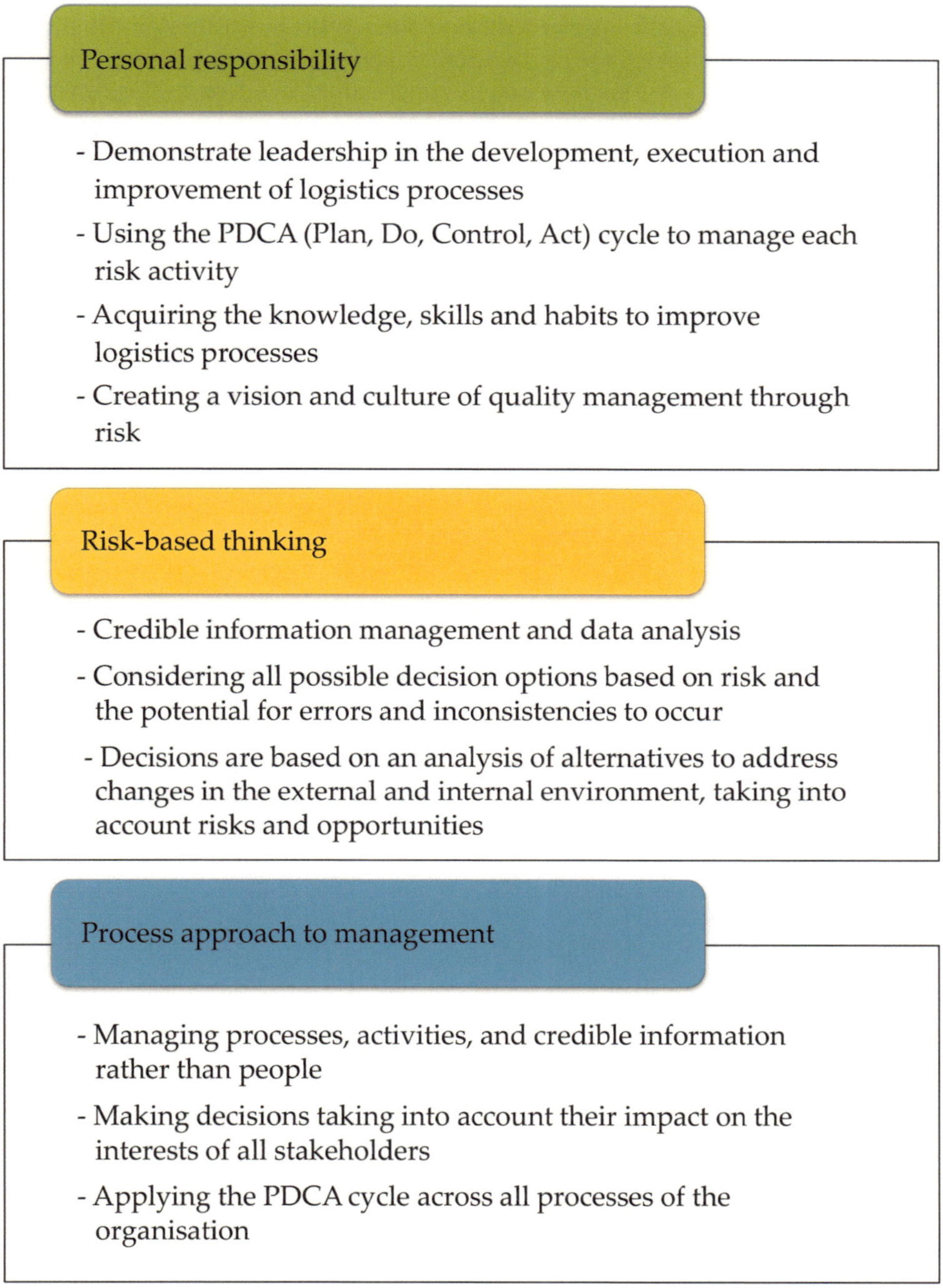

Figure 6.
Logical service quality management through leadership.

The financial responsibility for earnings management should rest with the department that has broader authority in making strategic decisions about target market definition, pricing policy, and asset management. It is good practice for this centre to make decisions on whether to outsource activities that are not typical and profitable for the organisation and hire, lease, or acquire the means of transport to perform the logistics services. It is unlikely that these centres will decide on funding sources and the basic nomenclature of logistics activities.

The financial investment management function has the greatest responsibility in the organisation and oversees the strategic effectiveness of logistics. The centre is the line decision-maker in selecting potential funding sources and determining directions, has the authority to manage assets.

The investment management department should define the risk management framework at each level of the organisation (**Figure 6**). The main aspects of focus are as follows:

- Understanding that the organisational context is the basic requirement for designing the risk management framework and defining risk levels and treatment criteria.
- Risk management principles are part of the logistics organisation's policy.
- Active internal communication between departments and control of documented information is used to communicate how risks and opportunities are being addressed.
- Adequate allocation of responsibilities and authority in actions to address risks and opportunities.
- The highest management level must ensure that:
- Risk management principles are part of the logistics service quality management policy.
- Based on its defined scope of organisational logistics activities, it formulates specific tasks to address risks and opportunities as part of the organisation's performance indicators.
- The defined framework and allocated responsibilities and powers are adequate to manage the framework.
- The resources provided and secured in the logistics activity to address risks and opportunities are adequate to the size and magnitude of the risks managed.
- Effective communication is applied to explain benefits and uncover beneficial opportunities in the interest of all stakeholders.
- Adequate actions are implemented to address quality management risks.

3. Actions to address risks and opportunities

Actions to address risks and opportunities are part of the logistics decision-making process at every level of the organisation and are a fundamental mechanism for quality improvement and management. The risks studied by the experts are labelled from F1 to F100 and acquire different numerical values according to the methodology set out in Chapter 2. The results of stages 4–8 are tabulated and included in Section 3.1 of the study.

3.1 Risk analysis of inefficient process management and human resource management

Shortage of human resources (F4) and lack of skills (F1), experience, and competence in logistics have been identified as two key factors contributing negatively to competitive advantage [14–18]. Along with these key factors, we witness increased staff turnover (F2) due to insufficient material incentives and management [19, 20]. First, to analyse the risk of process and human resource management, the study identifies how perceived problems, uncertainties, trends, and solutions are handled in the daily employee management during process management. The risks (F1 to F10) listed in the following tables and graphs provide a basis for further building plans to minimise or manage them in the field of real logistics. Very often, these risks are ignored by the management of the logistics company and subsequently become the cause of the shrinking or increasing losses of the activity. The risk associated with the lack of skilled labour [21] should be addressed by increasing the effectiveness of training (F3). Training programmes should be tailored to the different levels of staff competence attained [22, 23]. However, according to the experts involved in the study, it is often schematic and too general, and without a specific focus on the real problems arising in day-to-day work. The risks are magnified and exacerbated when company management does not provide a sufficient budget for staff training. In the wake of the pandemic, which necessitated social distance and limited commuting activities, logistics firms faced the challenge of dealing with reduced or limited human resources due to staff morbidity (F6). Evidently, emerging risks are related to a lack of professional interest, motivation to perform [24] and complete tasks, and mismatch between the employee's and the organisation's goals. Many researchers have proposed specific models for their management, including McAfee, Kilibarda, Anastasia, Kompf, Kanev, and others [25–31]. The main implications of risks related to process management and human resource management are summarised in **Table 1**.

Consequences	Initial PRN (Figure 7)					Actions to manage risks and opportunities	Residual PRN (Figure 8)				
	No	T	B	O	PRN		No	T	B	O	PRN
The absence of staff competence to perform a specific assigned task	F1	9	7	8	504	Periodic analysis and review of staff competency requirements	F1	9	5	8	360
Increasing staff turnover	F2	6	6	4	144	Improve the recruitment process (recruitment of trainees)	F2	6	4	5	120
Reducing the effectiveness of training	F3	9	6	6	324	Expansion of programmes and forms of training.	F3	9	3	6	162
Shortage of personnel to meet the requirements associated with the task.	F4	9	7	7	441	Improve the recruitment process (recruitment of trainees)	F4	9	6	7	378

Consequences	Initial PRN (Figure 7)					Actions to manage risks and opportunities	Residual PRN (Figure 8)				
	No	T	B	O	PRN		No	T	B	O	PRN
Lack of budget for staff training.	F5	5	8	3	120	Annual budget planning	F5	5	6	3	90
Temporary physical and mental disability of the employee	F6	6	6	2	72	Conduct preventive health check-ups	F6	6	5	2	60
Lack of professional interest and motivation to perform and complete the task	F7	7	4	9	252	Improved staff motivation system; Improved staff appraisal process	F7	7	3	9	189
Misalignment between the employee's personal goals and the organisation	F8	7	5	5	175	Career growth planning; Improving working conditions	F8	7	5	2	70
The appearance of conflict in the performance of assigned work	F9	7	5	6	210	Improved staff appraisal process.	F9	7	5	5	175

Table 1.
Risk analysis in process management and human resource management.

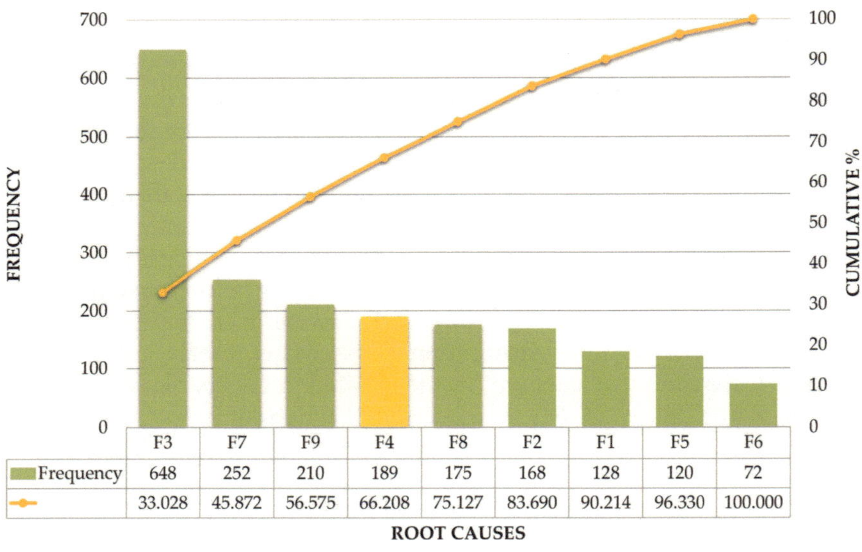

Figure 7.
Pareto analysis of initial PRN from F1 to F9.

In the analysis, the risk factor rated as the highest priority risk was the absence of staff competency to perform a specific assigned task (504) and after taking risk management actions, the risk of the residual PRN decreased (360). The new priority risk is to improve the process for searching and recruiting staff with PRN (378).

4. Analysis of risks associated with maintaining infrastructure and equipment

Logistics organisations must daily minimise the risk and impact of unforeseen damaging events associated with maintaining infrastructure and equipment. It does not

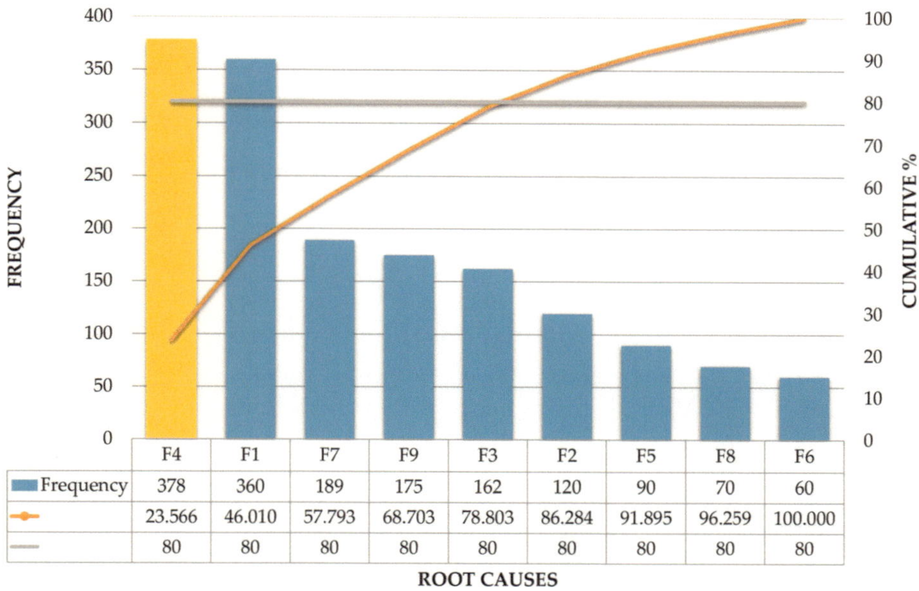

Figure 8.
Pareto analysis of residual PRN from F1 to F9.

need to be proven that a damaged transport vehicle could not complete the delivery. Therefore, various events, as well as inconsistent logistics and transport processes, may contribute to a deterioration in the quality of logistics services. Many researchers recommend various programmes or specific actions to minimise this risk [32, 33]. One potential solution is to implement an incentive model that can be utilised for scenario-based collaborative risk management [34, 35]. The main risks associated with infrastructure and equipment maintenance management are summarised in **Table 2**.

Consequences of risk	Initial PRN (Figure 9)					Actions to manage risks and opportunities	Residual PRN (Figure 10)				
	No	T	B	O	PRN		No	T	B	O	PRN
Failure of equipment or inadequate conditions for storage activities and infrastructure	F10	9	6	5	270	Improving the planning of repair and maintenance activities	F10	**8**	**3**	5	**120**
Failure to meet the schedule for infrastructure maintenance	F11	**8**	**4**	5	**160**	Establishing workable equipment maintenance schedules in coordination with external suppliers	F11	7	3	4	84
Failure to meet the repair schedule due to lack of qualified persons	F12	**8**	5	**6**	**240**	Increasing the competence of the staff carrying out the repair work or selecting a new provider for these services	F12	7	5	5	175
Shortage of material resources (technical equipment for the implementation of the process)	F13	**9**	**8**	**6**	**432**	Resource planning and improvement of technical equipment	F13	5	5	6	150

Consequences of risk	Initial PRN (Figure 9)					Actions to manage risks and opportunities	Residual PRN (Figure 10)				
	No	T	B	O	PRN		No	T	B	O	PRN
Repetitive failures, repetitive repairs	F14	**6**	**7**	**5**	**210**	Adjustment of the depreciation plan and life of the equipment	F14	**6**	**4**	**4**	**96**

Table 2.
Analysis of risks related to infrastructure and equipment maintenance.

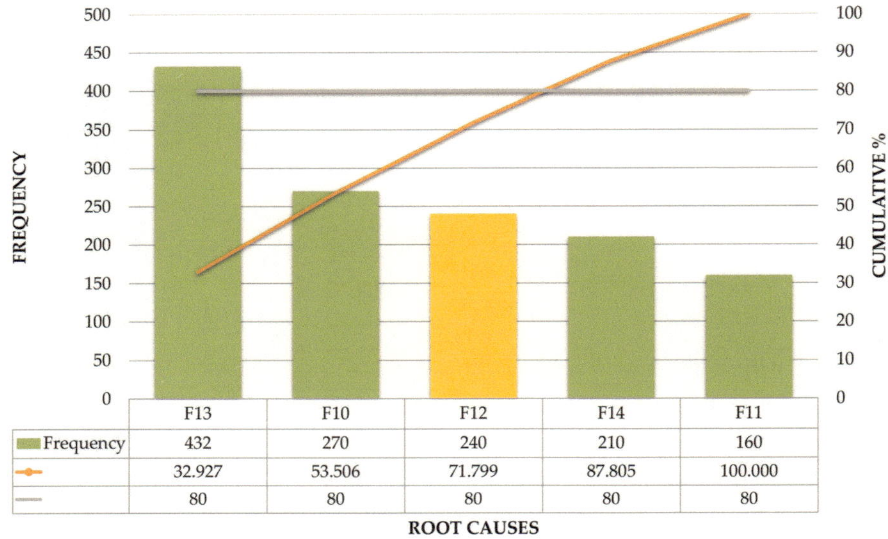

Figure 9.
Pareto analysis of initial PRN from F10 to F14.

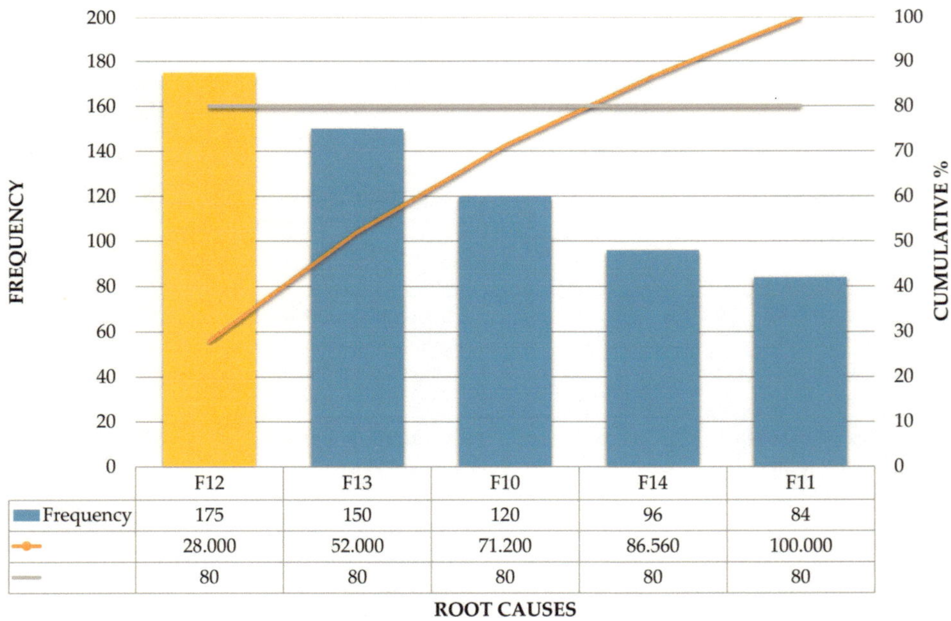

Figure 10.
Pareto analysis of residual PRN from F10 to F14.

In the analysis, the risk factor assessed with the highest priority risk was a shortage of material resources to perform the process (432) and after taking the risk management actions, the residual PRN has decreased to 150. The new priority risk is from failure to meet the schedule for repairs due to a lack of skilled personnel (PRN 175).

5. Managing risks associated with process control, monitoring, and measurement tools

Almost every logistics activity involves inventory management and inventory control. This necessitates the use of various monitoring and measurement tools that are affordably reliable to accurately account for the monitored items. The main activities involving monitoring and measuring tools are counting stock and collecting information on quantities of goods ordered, on hand, and dispatched. Some of the commodities handled in logistics must be stored under certain temperature and humidity conditions. Undoubtedly, if the measuring equipment did not correctly report these parameters and action was not taken when deviations from these parameters occurred, the company would suffer huge losses. The decision on what constitutes the appropriate means of measurement is based on each activity. Even when the means of measuring temperature is sufficiently reliable, it may not be suitable for the usage conditions. For example, thermometers that monitor temperature fluctuations in storage conditions in vehicles are not suitable for use in storage areas. The most complex task associated with measurement tools for inventory management is the purchase of a good data management system [36, 37] that processes the transaction data and generates reports and analyses in real time [38]. Many studies solve this problem; some researchers have also studied the existing inventory and stock management systems with their advantages and disadvantages [39–42, 43]. Choosing the right measurement tool for stock and inventory can help to improve the efficiency and execution of timely deliveries [44] while fully utilising the capacity of the delivery vehicle and warehouse. The main risks are maintaining optimal inventories under dynamically fluctuating order and delivery schedules [45–47], managing stock build-up in the warehouse as a result of fluctuations in demand [48], inadequate performance of logistics services when warehouses and transport facilities are not fully utilised [49], and containers for international transport [50]. The utilisation of full vehicle capacity deteriorates due to poor demand planning if the vehicle is empty in one direction for longer distance deliveries [51]. An interesting study by Wantanakomol optimises the decisions taken related to the sizing of delivery batches according to demand forecasting and inventory level [52].

Table 3 summarises the main risks of inefficient process management and management of monitoring and measurement tools.

Consequences	Initial PRN (Figure 11)					Actions to manage risks and opportunities	Residual PRN (Figure 12)				
	No	T	B	O	PRN		No	T	B	O	PRN
Control, monitoring and measurement error (biased control)	F15	**6**	**8**	**4**	**192**	Improve methods for identification and verification of measuring equipment	F15	**6**	**7**	**4**	**168**

Consequences	Initial PRN (Figure 11)					Actions to manage risks and opportunities	Residual PRN (Figure 12)				
	No	**T**	**B**	**O**	**PRN**		**No**	**T**	**B**	**O**	**PRN**
Performing control with untested or uncalibrated measuring equipment (biased control)	F16	**9**	**6**	**3**	**162**	Periodic review of monitoring and measurement techniques and methods	F16	5	4	3	**60**
Measurement uncertainty (high uncertainty of process measurement)	F17	7	5	2	**70**	Improve methods for identification and verification of measuring equipment	F17	7	3	2	**42**
Failure to comply with measurement conditions (temperature range, humidity)	F18	7	3	2	**42**	Improve methods for identification and verification of measuring equipment	F18	7	3	2	**42**
Incorrect interpretation of measurement results	F19	7	4	6	**168**	Improve competence of those carrying out monitoring and measurement	F19	7	4	3	**84**
Damage to measuring equipment during the measurement	F20	5	3	8	**120**	Availability of spare measuring equipment	F20	5	3	4	**60**
Damage to measuring equipment during transportation	F21	5	4	3	**60**	Periodic monitoring of ME storage and transport conditions	F21	5	4	3	**60**
Metering equipment failure incidents	F22	7	4	8	224	Occupational safety compliance programmes	F22	7	4	5	**140**

Table 3.
Risk analysis of inefficient process management: management of monitoring and measurement tools.

In the analysis, the risk factor assessed with the highest priority risk was incidents related to meter equipment failure (224), after taking the actions to manage the risk the residual PRN has decreased (140). The new priority risk is control, monitoring, and measurement Error (biased control) with a PRN of 168. Decisions to purchase new and more appropriate controls and process management software must be made considering the potential benefits, to the logistics firm and its customers, from the joint use of inventory control and warehouse management system in constrained systems.

6. Risk management of organisational knowledge

Organisational knowledge management risks arise from the contradiction that organisational knowledge is acquired, developed, and can be disseminated by employees, and logistics organisations can only create the necessary condition for defining, expanding, and protecting the malicious leakage of this knowledge. Nonaka has made great progress in defining a framework for organisational knowledge creation, which has been referenced by others 28,000 times [53]. Many researchers have conducted and, consequently, published studies on the positive effect in the

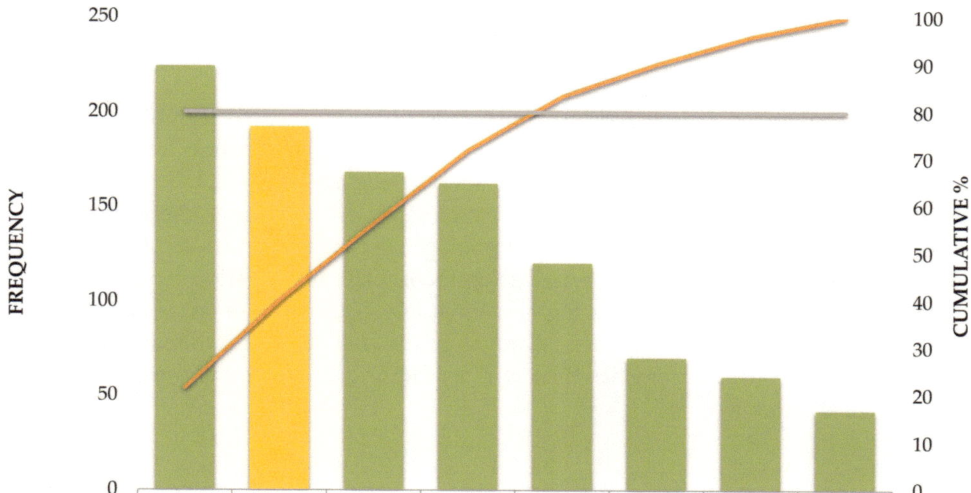

	F22	F15	F19	F16	F20	F17	F21	F18
Frequency	224	192	168	162	120	70	60	42
	21.580	40.077	56.262	71.869	83.430	90.173	95.954	100.000
	80	80	80	80	80	80	80	80

ROOT CAUSES

Figure 11.
Pareto analysis of initial PRN from F15 to F22.

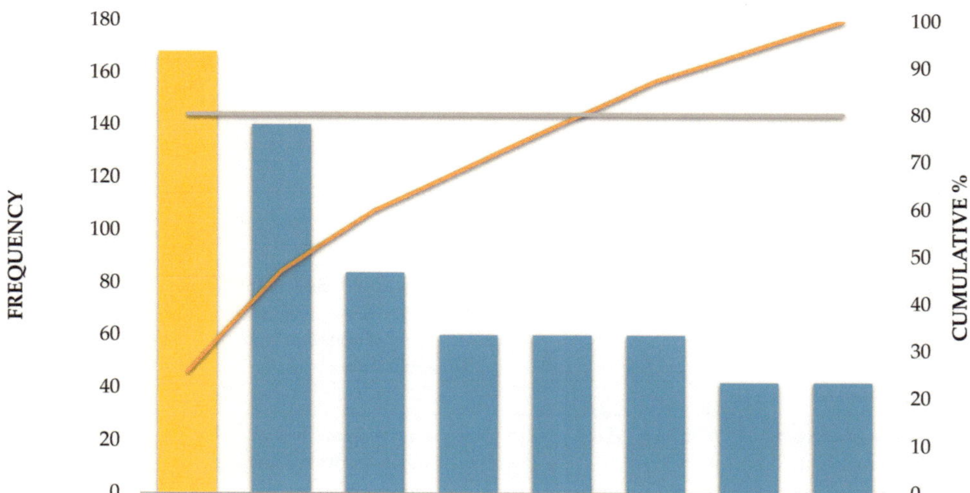

	F15	F22	F19	F16	F20	F21	F17	F18
Frequency	168	140	84	60	60	60	42	42
	25.610	46.951	59.756	68.902	78.049	87.195	93.598	100.000
	80	80	80	80	80	80	80	80

ROOT CAUSES

Figure 12.
Pareto analysis of residual PRN from F15 to F22.

management of knowledge sharing but the negative effect of knowledge leakage, including knowledge in the management of logistics processes, are still not adequately studied. There has been extensive research on the impact of protecting knowledge and information by developing a portfolio of measures [54–58]. A summary of the risks of ineffective management of the organisational knowledge management process is presented in **Table 4**.

Experts assigned the highest priority risk scores to two factors—lack of information to analyse the problem and use of incomplete information from the organisation's database. After actions were taken to manage the risk, the residual PRN decreased from 405 to 225 for the first factor and 432 to 288 for the second. Despite the actions and measures taken to manage risks, the risk factors of not having information to analyse the problem and using incomplete information from the organisation's database remain at a high level, which requires these factors to be monitored as a priority in the future. Minimising the risk of organisational knowledge leakage is essential for any logistics firm as a key factor in maintaining the organisation's competitive advantage.

Consequences	**Initial PRN (Figure 13)**					**Actions to manage risks and opportunities**	**Residual PRN (Figure 14)**				
	No	**T**	**B**	**O**	**PRN**		**No**	**T**	**B**	**O**	**PRN**
Leakage of information from the organisation's database.	F23	9	5	8	360	Increase the organisation's information security, implement ISO/IEC 27001:2013.	F23	9	3	7	189
Dissemination of false information within the organisation	F24	9	5	7	315	Preparation and periodic updating of the list of the organisation's information assets	F24	9	4	6	216
Lack of information to analyse the problem.	F25	9	5	9	405	Involve experts to develop the database in the organisation	F25	9	5	5	225
Lack of information needed to solve the problem.	F26	10	7	3	210	Improve the system for collecting and analysing data from external sources	F26	10	6	3	180
Deliberate dissemination of inapplicable information and knowledge within the organisation.	F27	9	4	3	108	Conduct an expert assessment of the currency, completeness, and order of information from the organisation's banking sources	F27	9	3	3	81
Unauthorised use and dissemination of information in the organisation's knowledge base.	F28	9	5	4	180	Increase motivation through information security training in the organisation	F28	5	2	4	40
Use of incomplete information from the organisation's database.	F29	9	8	6	432	Conduct expert assessment of the update, completion, and order of use of information from the organisation's banking sources; Conduct expert assessment and document control prior to approval.	F29	6	8	6	288

Table 4.
Ineffective process management.

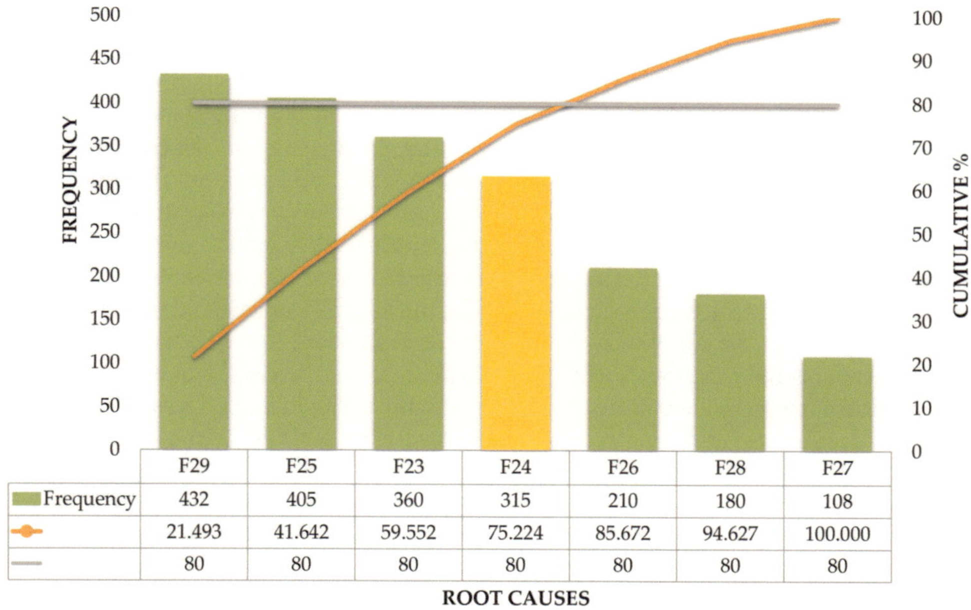

	F29	F25	F23	F24	F26	F28	F27
Frequency	432	405	360	315	210	180	108
	21.493	41.642	59.552	75.224	85.672	94.627	100.000
	80	80	80	80	80	80	80

Figure 13.
Pareto chart analysis of initial PRN from F23 to F29.

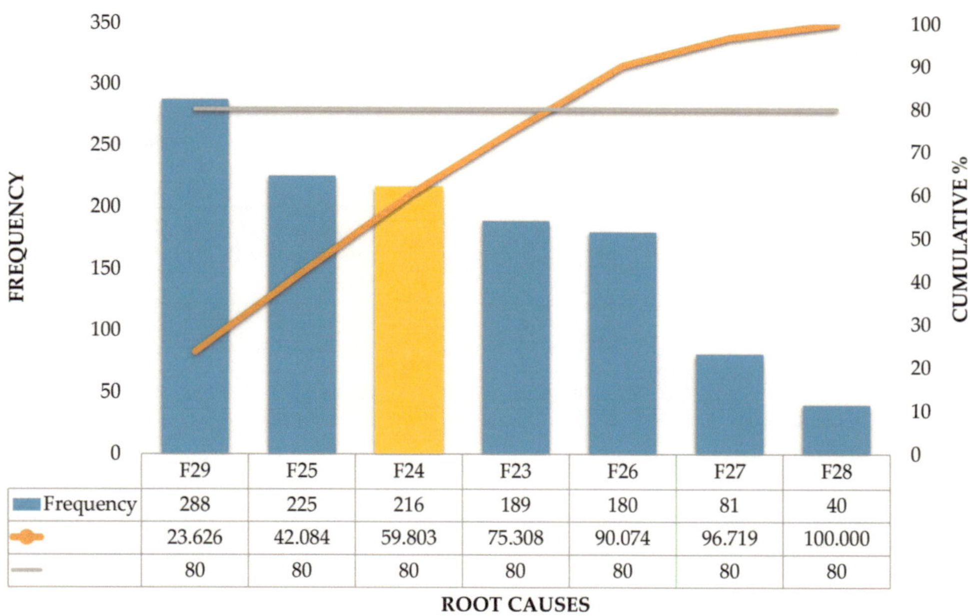

	F29	F25	F24	F23	F26	F27	F28
Frequency	288	225	216	189	180	81	40
	23.626	42.084	59.803	75.308	90.074	96.719	100.000
	80	80	80	80	80	80	80

Figure 14.
Pareto chart analysis of residual PRN from F23 to F29.

7. Management of documented information

Achieving quality in logistics operations requires documented information on the status of the units to be managed at each stage of the process and transport of goods between logistics warehouses. This flow of information becomes larger and more complex as the product physically approaches the end user. In recent years, with the free movement of goods, the required information documentation accompanying the goods has become more detailed and voluminous. Many researchers have explored the strategic potential of effective interaction between logistics and information technology for customer value creation and process performance management [59–64]. Some researchers have also proposed specific models to manage and promote the implementation of an effective sustainability risk management system in the logistics network [56, 65–68]. These prerequisites create risks that must be managed to prevent the destruction, total loss, or tampering of documented information between logistics operators and manufacturers or customers. The most significant risk, identified by the experts involved in the study, was the inconsistencies related to the complexity of the requirements or the competence of the staff to process them and the loss of documented information during the execution of logistics activities. The increased risk of loss of transport documents has been investigated by several researchers, some of whom have suggested specific improvements to minimise this impact [69–73]. Achieving a higher quality of logistics services can be sought through the creation of an adequate documented information management system, which has the potential to contribute and solve the ongoing tasks of delivering various goods just in time and prevent and reduce possible logistics loss risks in the future. **Table 5** presents the results of the risk analysis related to the ineffective management of documented information.

In the analysis conducted, the risk factor rated with the highest priority risk was the loss of documented information (504); after actions were taken to manage the risk, the residual PRN decreased (324). The new priority risk is a breach of confidentiality of documented information with PRN (378).

Consequences	Initial PRN (Figure 15)					Actions to manage risks and opportunities	Residual PRN (Figure 16)				
	No	T	B	O	PRN		No	T	B	O	PRN
Incorrect or incomplete completion of record forms.	F30	9	6	4	216	Timely updating and programming of documented information	F30	8	5	4	160
Records management errors.	F31	6	5	4	120	Control of training on documented information	F31	4	5	4	80
The use of outdated documented information (including that of external origin).	F32	9	8	4	288	Improve methods for managing documents of internal and external origin, including search engines	F32	8	8	4	256
Inconsistency in documented staffing, competency, and/or complexity of requirements.	F33	9	6	5	270	Increase information security in accordance with ISO 27001:2013 requirements	F33	9	5	5	225
Lack of access to the full set of documents at the point of use.	F34	9	7	7	441	Preparation and periodic updating of the list of the organisation's information assets	F34	9	6	3	162
Delayed receipt of documented information.	F35	9	8	7	504	Prepare and periodically update the organisation's information assets	F35	9	6	6	324

Consequences	Initial PRN (Figure 15)					Actions to manage risks and opportunities	Residual PRN (Figure 16)				
	No	T	B	O	PRN		No	T	B	O	PRN
Lack of documented information.	F36	9	6	5	270	Timely software and database updates	F36	9	5	5	225
Loss of documented information	F37	9	7	5	315	Improving document management methods	F37	9	7	3	189
Breach of confidentiality of documented information.	F38	9	8	6	432	Increase motivation through information security training in the organisation	F38	9	7	6	378

Table 5.
Management of documented information.

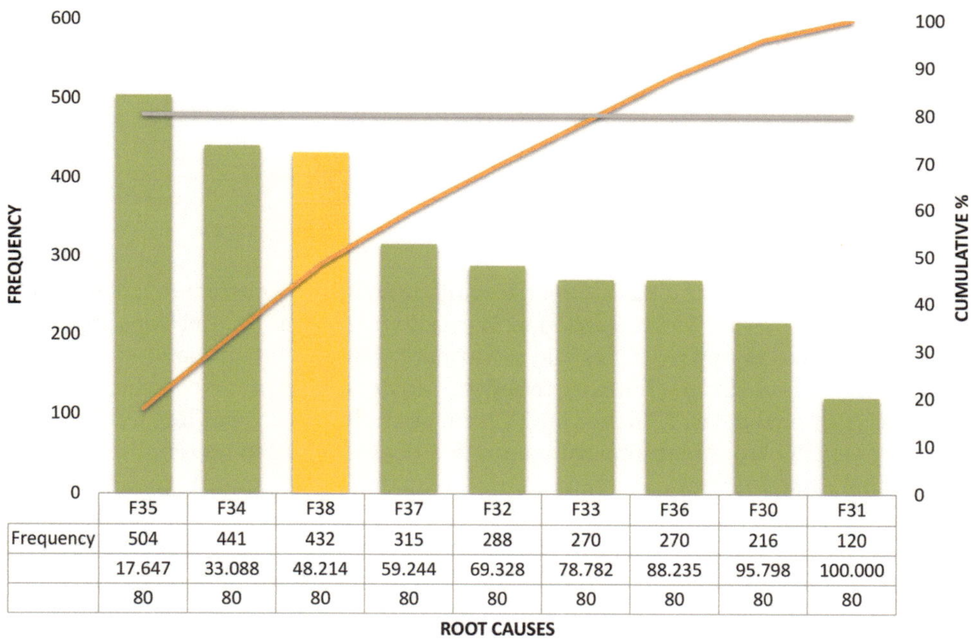

	F35	F34	F38	F37	F32	F33	F36	F30	F31
Frequency	504	441	432	315	288	270	270	216	120
	17.647	33.088	48.214	59.244	69.328	78.782	88.235	95.798	100.000
	80	80	80	80	80	80	80	80	80

Figure 15.
Pareto analysis of initial PRN from F30 to F38.

8. Ineffective process management: marketing (including customer communication)

The link between logistics activities and marketing must be made in line with the decision-making for each specific logistics service. Marketing activities are linked to decision-making not only on how to deliver the products but also the choice of the types of outlets where the products will be delivered and the form in which sales will take place. Particular attention should be paid to promotional activities. Internet commerce has developed at a significant pace in recent years, which has also allowed potential business opportunities to grow. The policy chosen for the distribution of

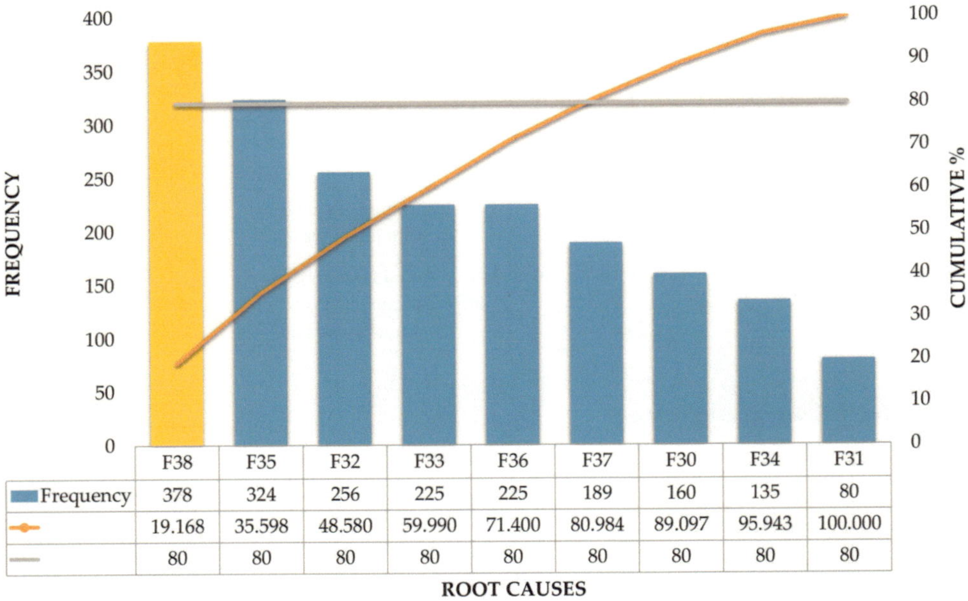

	F38	F35	F32	F33	F36	F37	F30	F34	F31
Frequency	378	324	256	225	225	189	160	135	80
	19.168	35.598	48.580	59.990	71.400	80.984	89.097	95.943	100.000
	80	80	80	80	80	80	80	80	80

Figure 16.
Pareto analysis of residual PRN from F30 to F38.

goods is a high priority and has a direct bearing on increasing customer satisfaction with logistics services. The integration of logistics and marketing functions allows the expansion of market opportunities and assortment. Internal integration between logistics processes helps to eliminate functional errors and improve coordination between functional areas. Gimenez and Ventura's study on external integration of logistics [74] concludes that internal integration does not lead to better absolute performance and does not contribute to cost reduction, production availability, or lead time (the article has been cited over 650 times). Flynn's study [75] builds on this view by exploring the reasons for the lack of positive effect and demonstrates that the integration approach needs to be contingency-driven. His study concludes that internal and customer integration are more strongly associated with performance improvement than supplier integration.

Experts find that the highest risk in this area is an unidentified properly positioned market segment and capacity. To minimise this risk, organisations must reorient logistics services to customers who contribute the most and have the greatest potential for growth, while reducing or even eliminating customers who do not contribute to prosperity. The inconsistency with the greatest negative effect is the acceptance by logistics organisations that the market is homogeneous, and the same services are provided to different groups of customers who have different backgrounds and different logistics needs. **Table 6** presents the results of the risk analysis related to Ineffective Process Management: Marketing.

In the analysis, the risk factor assessed with the highest priority risk was the failure to satisfy customer requirements in the long term (720); after actions were taken to manage the risk, the residual PRN has decreased (648). One of the consequences of the risks is related to the insufficient expansion of the range of services offered and failure to provide new and innovative logistics services. As a result of being

Consequences	Initial PRN (Figure 17)					Actions to manage risks and opportunities	Residual PRN (Figure 18)				
	No	T	B	O	PRN		No	T	B	O	PRN
Shortage of marketing department staff with competence to solve marketing problems	F39	10	9	4	360	Improves the employee search and recruitment process (hiring trainees) and periodic competency analysis of marketing department staff	F39	9	9	4	324
Omission of commercial information	F40	9	7	8	504	Increase the competence of the marketing department staff, including training, internship program	F40	8	7	8	448
Lack of budget for marketing activities	F41	8	6	3	144	Improve the planning of marketing activities and increase the frequency of execution of plans	F41	7	6	3	126
Lack of motivation and effective communication between the client and the organisation	F42	8	8	2	128	Analysis of communication channels	F42	8	7	2	112
Loss of brand loyalty	F43	9	7	6	378	Improve marketing activity planning	F43	9	7	6	378
Market segment and positioning capacity not properly identified	F44	10	7	9	630	Improve marketing activity planning	F44	10	5	8	400
Ignoring internal communication at the expense of external	F45	9	6	6	324	Improve internal communication between departments	F45	9	6	5	270
Customer relationship management only, without considering the entire supply chain	F46	10	8	8	640	Improve planning with consideration of the entire supply chain	F46	9	8	6	432
Underestimate the potential of emerging markets	F47	8	9	9	648	Improve planning to consider the potential of emerging markets	F47	8	9	7	504
Satisfy unrealistic demands that are important for the logistics company but not for the customer	F48	10	8	7	560	Improve planning with consideration of actual customer requirements	F48	9	8	6	432
Failure to meet customer requirements in the long term	F49	10	9	8	720	Improve planning with consideration of actual customer requirements	F49	9	9	8	648
Lack of expansion of the range of services offered and failure to provide innovative logistics service	F50	10	9	7	630	Improving planning to consider innovation in the sector	F50	9	9	7	567

Table 6.
Ineffective process management: marketing.

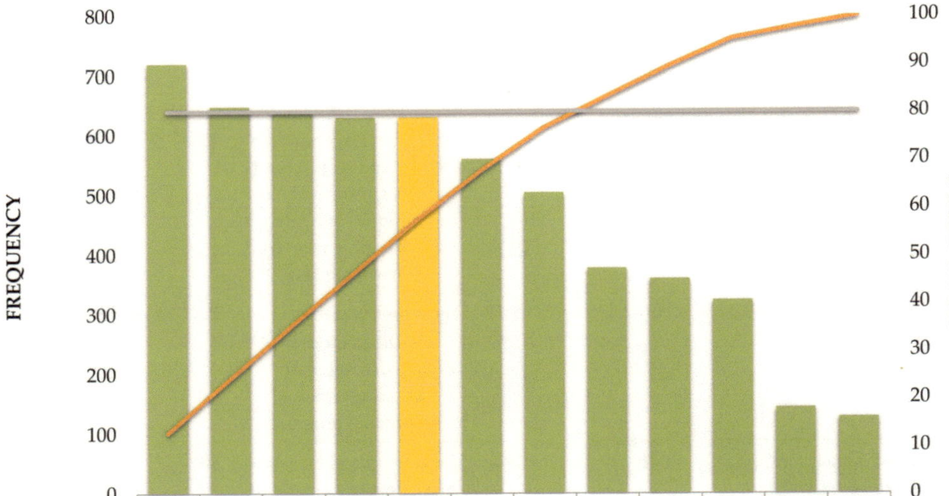

	F49	F47	F46	F44	F50	F48	F40	F43	F39	F45	F41	F42
Frequency	720	648	640	630	630	560	504	378	360	324	144	128
	12.707	24.144	35.439	46.558	57.677	67.561	76.456	83.127	89.481	95.199	97.741	100.00
	80	80	80	80	80	80	80	80	80	80	80	80

ROOT CAUSES

Figure 17.
Pareto analysis of initial PRN from F39 to F50.

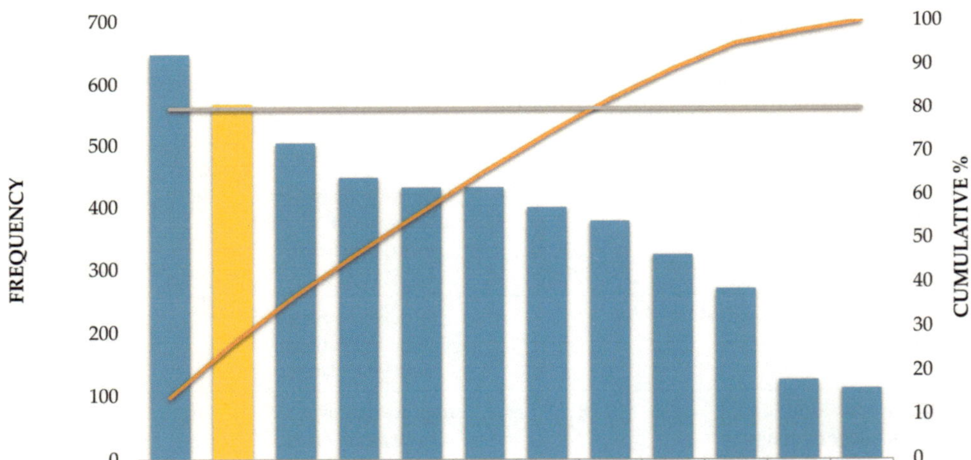

	F49	F50	F47	F40	F46	F48	F44	F43	F39	F45	F41	F42
Frequency	648	567	504	448	432	432	400	378	324	270	126	112
	13.963	26.180	37.039	46.693	56.001	65.309	73.928	82.073	89.054	94.872	97.587	100.00
	80	80	80	80	80	80	80	80	80	80	80	80

ROOT CAUSES

Figure 18.
Pareto analysis of residual PRN from F39 to F50.

reclassified from fifth in priority to second, the logistics organisation's efforts must be directed towards its priority monitoring with minimisation of risk consequences (PRN 567).

9. Ineffective process management: contract analysis

The rapid development of logistics services does not correspond to standard contracts for freight forwarding, logistics, and transport. Many researchers have identified emerging issues between the service offered, its legal function, and the risk of sales uncertainty associated with the transfer of ownership of goods and product liability to the logistics provider [76–79]. The main challenges are related to closer cooperation and relationship between the logistics company and the law firm, which establishes a contractual relationship with customers and defines the legal consequences. The inconsistencies in this process are related to the failure to understand the full legal impact and implications of even minor changes in the contractual relationship.

Contracts are an appropriate tool not only for managing logistics risks but also for managing customer relationships and for establishing and facilitating communication, coordination, motivation, and control between business partners. Well-managed contractual relationships can have a positive impact in preventing problems, reducing litigated claims, and regulating and governing relationships that would be difficult to achieve without contracts [80, 81]. The concepts of supply chain vulnerability and risk management require a more precise definition [82] by negotiating actions when incidents and emergencies occur.

Table 7 presents the results of a risk analysis related to ineffective process management: contract analysis.

Consequences	Initial PRN (Figure 19)					Actions to manage risks and opportunities	Residual PRN (Figure 20)				
	No	T	B	O	PRN		No	T	B	O	PRN
cExceeding the processing time for customer enquiries	F51	10	10	8	800	Improve methods for scheduling and handling customer enquiries	F51	10	10	6	600
Inconsistencies in the drafting of the contract	F52	10	8	7	560	Development and use of standard forms for contract drafts	F52	10	8	5	400
Incorrect expert opinion on the draft contract	F53	9	8	6	432	Increase the competence of the experts reviewing the contracts proposed for approval and simplify the contract drafting procedure	F53	9	7	4	252
Not all amendments are made when product (service) requirements change	F54	10	8	8	640	Use of corporate information systems for contract design and review	F54	10	7	7	490
Ineffective process of establishing long-term stable and trusting relationships with customers	F55	7	8	4	224	Increase the competence of the experts responsible for validating contracts and simplify the contract drafting procedure	F55	6	8	4	192
Underestimating the risk to the outcome of a lawsuit with non-compliant logistical processes	F56	9	7	6	378	Review of the actuality of the claims handling budget	F56	9	7	5	315

Consequences	Initial PRN (Figure 19)					Actions to manage risks and opportunities	Residual PRN (Figure 20)				
	No	T	B	O	PRN		No	T	B	O	PRN
Failure to take adequate and timely action to address complaints	F57	9	8	7	504	Develop a programme and procedure for dealing with complaints	F57	9	7	6	378
The occurrence of a risk in the supply chain that is beyond the company's control	F58	10	10	9	900	Establish a risk management and information control program and supply chain changes	F58	10	9	8	720
Changes to regulated rules on compensation for injuries and damages	F59	10	8	8	640	Establish a risk management and information control program and supply chain changes	F59	10	7	8	560
Changes to the rules governing forwarding agency and customs clearance	F60	10	9	8	720	Establish a risk management and information control program and supply chain changes	F60	10	7	8	560

Table 7.
Ineffective process management: contract analysis.

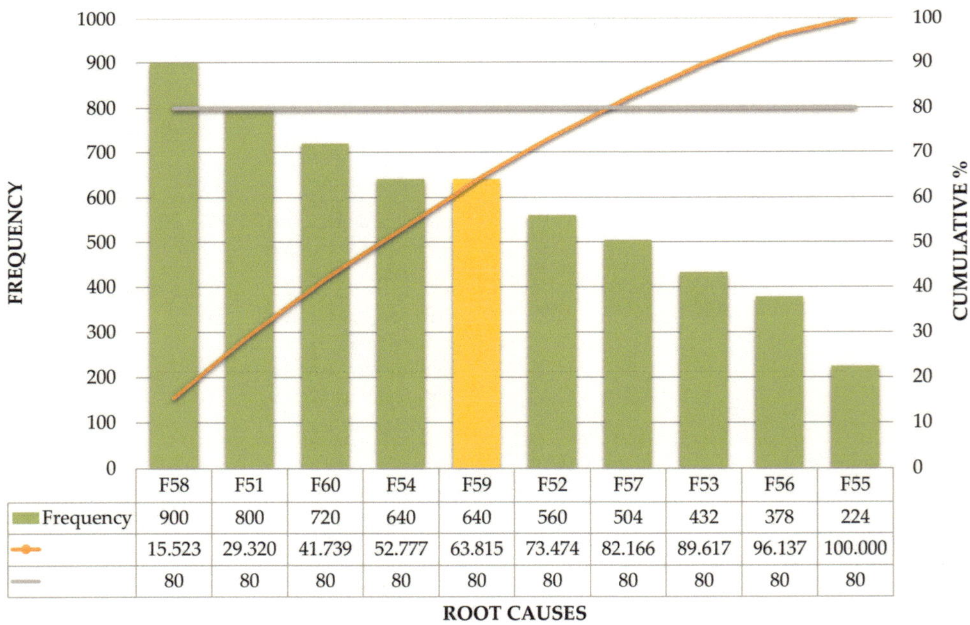

Figure 19.
Pareto analysis of initial PRN from F51 to F60.

To prevent these risks of legal claims and litigation and seek a path to effective resolution of disputes before they reach the courts, a legal framework should be established to regulate these relationships. The risk of not taking adequate and timely action to address claims was assessed as the greatest risk of non-compliance in the

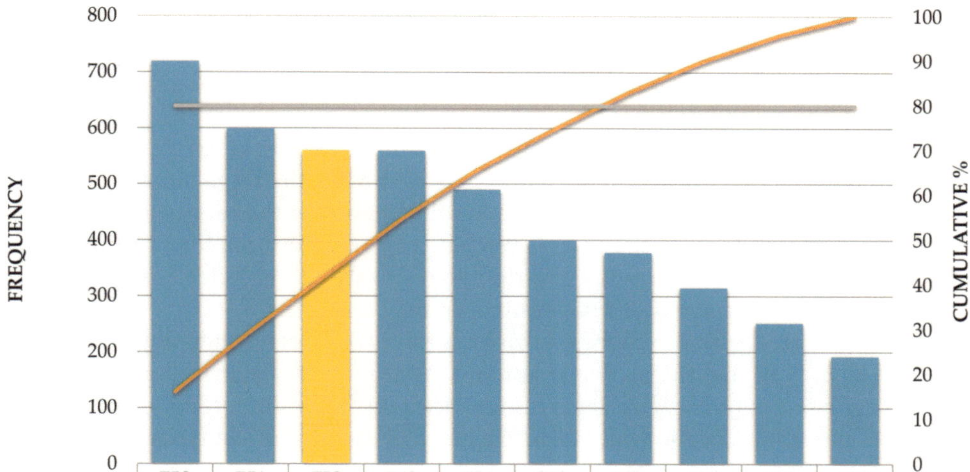

	F58	F51	F59	F60	F54	F52	F57	F56	F53	F55
Frequency	720	600	560	560	490	400	378	315	252	192
	16.118	29.550	42.086	54.623	65.592	74.547	83.009	90.060	95.702	100.000
	80	80	80	80	80	80	80	80	80	80

ROOT CAUSES

Figure 20.
Pareto analysis of residual PRN from F51 to F60.

process. In the analysis, the factor assessed with the highest priority risk was the occurrence of a supply chain risk that is outside the control of the organisation. Making adequate and informed decisions to minimise this risk should become a top priority for the organisation. The increased frequency and severe consequences of past supply chain disruptions, as witnessed during the COVID-19 pandemic, set the stage for the deterioration of many logistics organisations' financial performance.

The risk management actions set out in **Table 7** are about making appropriate decisions; however, their effect, similar to any event, is associated with a degree of uncertainty and indeterminacy. It should be noted that the process of taking action to manage any risk should be continuous because misjudgements of risk factors can lead to unforeseen developments that can have negative consequences when identified too late. The consequences will be greatest for logistics organisations with only one warehouse or only one single supply channel. To prevent these severe consequences of external risks from threatening the company's control, plans must be put in place to manage them and, if possible, move towards diversification before or as changes in the environment occur. This process becomes more difficult to manage when negative changes occur in the external environment. In such cases, risk factors may outweigh mitigation strategies. The occurrence of risks in the supply chain as a result of unpredictable events that occur suddenly and are high impact, which are not within the control of the company, can lead to the potential loss of the organisation's efficiency and effectiveness targets. Thus, the process of reassessing control measures for the most highly rated risk by experts must be continuously monitored and managed.

10. Inefficient process management: design and development of new services

Risk management issues in logistics projects are primarily related to resourcing. These problems can be resolved by introducing internationally accepted quality standards for risk management (ISO 9001; ISO 31000; ISO 31010) in project management by using a systematic approach. It is a globally accepted good practice to integrate risk management into corporate sustainability management as a stand-alone functional unit.

Resourcing can be provided through support contracts with resource providers to mitigate risk. The potential to significantly reduce risks in the implementation of project activities is defined by good logistical coordination in the receipt and execution of requests and rapid response to negative changes in the environment and supply chain. **Table 8** presents the results of a risk analysis related to ineffective process management in the design and development of new services.

The factor rated with the highest priority is failure to meet design objectives. It need not be proven that the management and resourcing of design logistics risks and risk management in operational logistics activities should be integrated to achieve the objectives and minimise the waste of resources. The risk of human resource shortage

Consequences	Initial PRN (Figure 21)					Actions to manage risks and opportunities	Residual PRN (Figure 22)				
	No	T	B	O	PRN		No	T	B	O	PRN
Failure to meet design objectives	F61	8	8	7	448	Enhancing competencies for the management and implementation of project activities	F61	8	6	7	336
Failure to meet the design deadline	F62	7	6	4	168	Improve planning methods	F62	7	4	4	112
Design cost over-runs	F63	7	5	4	140	Optimise the frequency and depth of analysis phases for design performance	F63	7	3	4	84
Shortage of material resources for the implementation of the logistics project	F64	9	3	5	135	Provide material resources or secure them through resource support contracts	F64	9	3	4	108
Shortage of human resources for the implementation of the logistics project	F65	10	10	4	400	Provision of human resources with employment programmes or through resource support contracts with organisations providing this type of service	F65	10	8	4	320
Shortage of material resources for the implementation of the logistics project	F66	6	5	6	180	Ensure financial resources or secure them through resource support agreements with lending institutions	F66	6	5	4	120
Lack of financial resources to implement the logistics project	F67	5	4	5	100	Provide material resources or secure them through resource support contracts	F67	5	2	5	50
Unproductive processes that hinder project implementation	F68	4	4	4	64	Optimise the frequency and depth of analysis phases for design performance	F68	4	4	4	64
Implementation of processes that do not add value	F69	6	5	6	180	Optimise the frequency and depth of analysis phases for design performance	F69	6	4	6	144

Consequences	Initial PRN (Figure 21)					Actions to manage risks and opportunities	Residual PRN (Figure 22)				
	No	T	B	O	PRN		No	T	B	O	PRN
Poor coordination between the members of the logistics project team	F70	7	8	5	280	Actions to increase coordination: workshops and operational meetings	F70	7	8	3	168

Table 8.
Ineffective process management: design and development of new services.

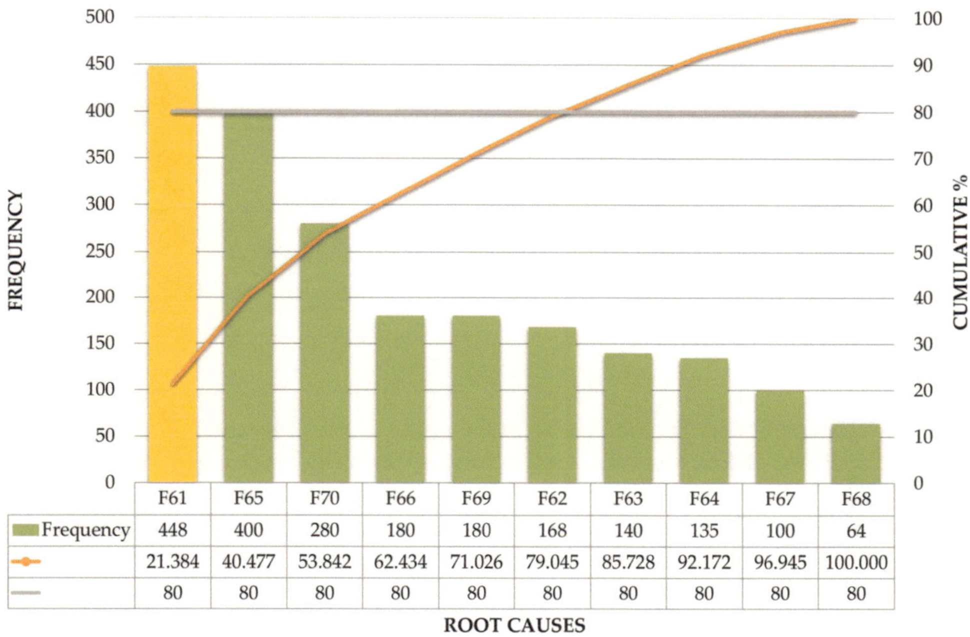

Figure 21.
Pareto analysis of initial PRN from F61 to F70.

for logistics project implementation is highly appreciated. In addition to resourcing logistics projects, there is a need to establish a mechanism and develop programs to manage the vulnerability of project activities and implications for management throughout the implementation chain, while eliminating unproductive activities that do not add value to the organisation or customers.

11. Inefficient process management: management of processes, products, and services by external suppliers

The processes and products provided to the organisation by external suppliers are driven by the growing trend towards outsourcing of secondary logistics activities—transportation, packaging, and warehousing. The rationale for the demand for outsourcing logistics services is related to improving competitiveness by streamlining business activities and concentrating entirely on core competencies.

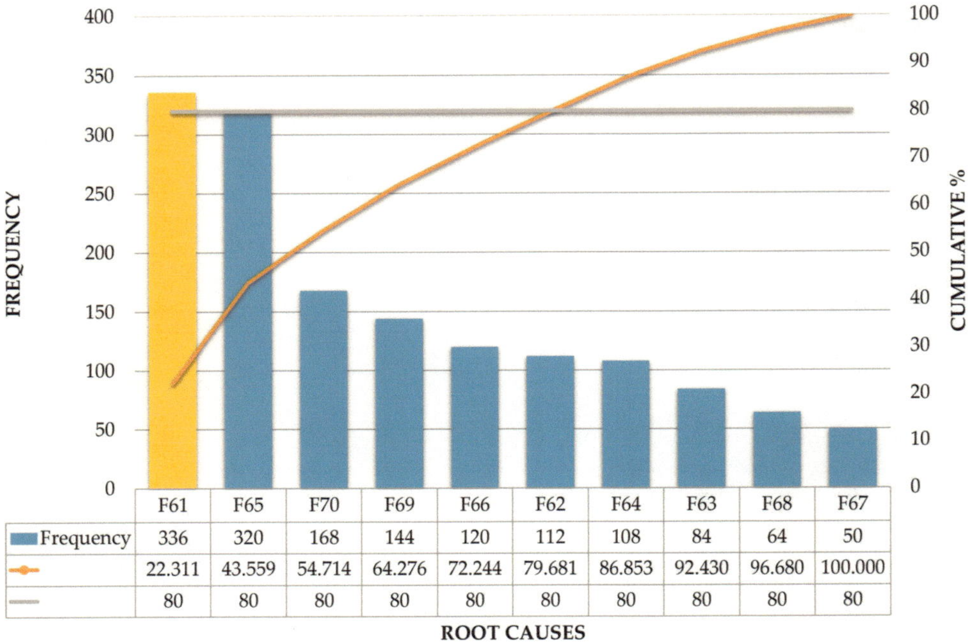

Figure 22.
Pareto analysis of residual PRN from F61 to F70.

Many researchers are focused on identifying the factors for reaching outsourcing selection decisions. Most research publications identify the following factors:

- access to expertise from classified staff and experts [83, 84].
- reduce or stabilise costs [85–87].
- concentrate on core competencies [88, 89].
- financial restructuring [90, 91].
- overcome organisational problems [92].

Table 9 presents the results of a risk analysis related to ineffective process management of processes, products, and services from external suppliers.

Consequences	Initial PRN (Figure 23)					Actions to manage risks and opportunities	Residual PRN (Figure 24)				
	No	T	B	O	PRN		No	T	B	O	PRN
Irregular deliveries	F71	10	8	9	720	Establish a supplier management program. Negotiate with alternative suppliers of the same commodity	F71	10	8	5	400

DOI: http://dx.doi.org/10.5772/intechopen.103755

Consequences	Initial PRN (Figure 23)					Actions to manage risks and opportunities	Residual PRN (Figure 24)				
	No	**T**	**B**	**O**	**PRN**		**No**	**T**	**B**	**O**	**PRN**
Lack of resources for effective supply planning	F72	8	7	4	224	Improve staff competency to execute project activities and pre-agree budget to meet objectives and Adequacy Analysis of design resources	F72	8	7	3	168
The impact of changes on the achievement of design objectives	F73	6	3	4	72	Analysis of all implications, introduction of changes as a result of the design	F73	6	3	4	72
Failure to meet delivery deadlines for external processes, products, and services	F74	10	7	9	630	Expand the list of approved suppliers and reduce the timeframe for their approval and validation	F74	10	7	8	560

Table 9.
Management of processes, products, and services from external suppliers.

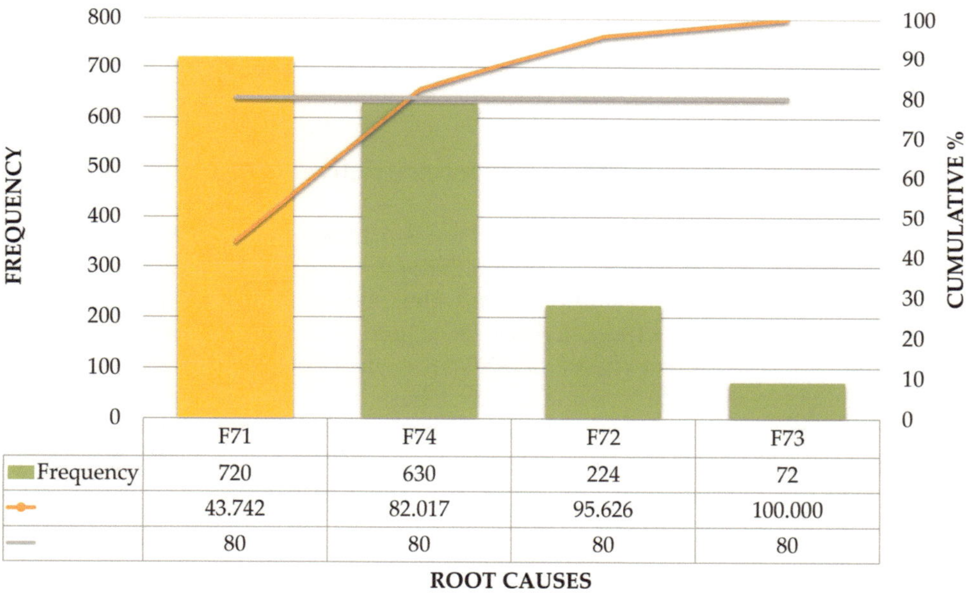

Figure 23.
Pareto analysis of initial PRN from F71 to F74.

Irregularity of supply has been identified as the greatest risk in processes related to services from external suppliers (PRN 720). This risk arises from the lack of control over processes that are under the supplier's control. Typically, the issues related to the supplier's management experience and skills, which may be less than expected, and their inability to meet the performance requirements for the services.

Lack of outsourced process supplier capability can also negatively impact the risk of missing delivery deadlines. After the action was taken to manage the risk and the potential impact of failure to meet delivery deadlines was assessed by the experts with high scores; the risk is now ranked as priority one.

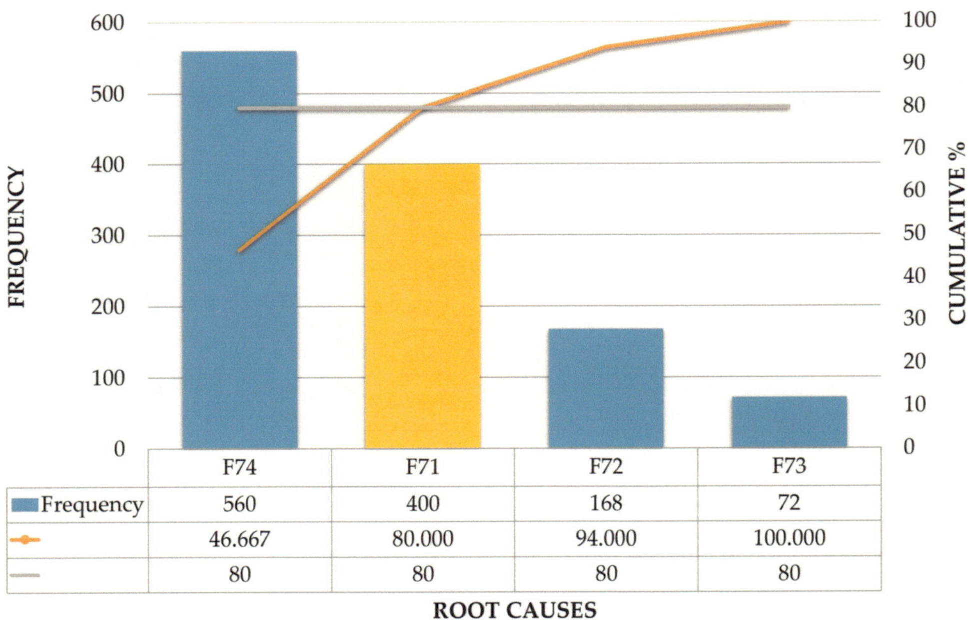

Figure 24.
Pareto analysis of residual PRN from F71 to F74.

12. Ineffective process management: service delivery

Logistics activities, such as inventory and order management, warehousing, and transportation, can be managed through the opportunities provided by technological developments to organise supply chain relationships. Customers have identified the timeliness of requested deliveries as one of the most significant factors in their satisfaction. The present study found that the quality of logistics services has significantly impacted satisfaction and loyalty. Thus, logistics organisations must invest resources to improve quality management and share these improvements throughout the supply chain. **Table 10** presents the results of the risk analysis on ineffective process management—external suppliers' processes, products, and services.

Consequences	Initial PRN (Figure 25)					Actions to manage risks and opportunities	Residual PRN (Figure 26)				
	No	T	B	O	PRN		No	T	B	O	PRN
Discrepancies between the characteristics of the services provided and those specified in the contract.	F75	10	7	6	420	Analyse the adequacy of resources for service delivery and expand the list of established outsourcing providers	F75	10	6	5	300
Error in the preparation of the proposed contracts to be agreed, including incomplete and incorrect information;	F76	10	4	4	160	Introduce a requirement to use legal advice to improve the wording of clauses in contracts with external suppliers	F76	10	3	4	120

Consequences	Initial PRN (Figure 25)					Actions to manage risks and opportunities	Residual PRN (Figure 26)				
	No	T	B	O	PRN		No	T	B	O	PRN
Inaccurate completion of the requirements for the characteristics of the products supplied and/or incomplete description of the service or process supplied.	F77	10	7	6	420	Improve the system for processing requests for products and services delivered	F77	10	6	6	360
Failure to meet a product or service delivery deadline.	F78	9	5	4	180	Regularly monitor and improve the service delivery techniques (technology documentation) and Improvement of planning methods	F78	9	3	4	108
Provision of service in breach of procedure or failure to comply with an established service provision procedure	F79	10	7	6	420	Training and competence of the process owner and operators	F79	10	4	6	240
Failure to comply with the general conditions laid down in the approved contracts	F80	10	4	4	160	Training and competency of process owner and operators and optimising the frequency and depth of management review in the service delivery process	F80	10	4	3	120
Lack of human and material resources for service delivery	F81	10	7	6	420	Resource adequacy analysis for service delivery	F81	10	5	4	200
The logistics services provided do not meet the agreed specification	F82	8	5	4	160	Training and competency of process owner and operators and optimising the frequency and depth of management review in the service delivery process	F82	8	4	4	128

Table 10.
Ineffective process management.

Several consequences of the risk are rated high by the experts (F75, F77, F79, and F81). Business planning and management software and resource and process optimisation may have a positive impact on improving the request process by facilitating and meeting delivery terms agreed with the customer. Business software to plan and manage transport activities may have a positive impact on the on-time delivery of orders by meeting the delivery deadline agreed with the customer (factors from F78, F80, and F82). The shortage of classified customer liaison staff in logistics is a growing risk and organisations should, therefore, focus on training and improving the skills of employees needed to provide a high level of customer service (F82). The organisation's management must address the shortage of human resources to execute processes along with specific actions to manage the risks.

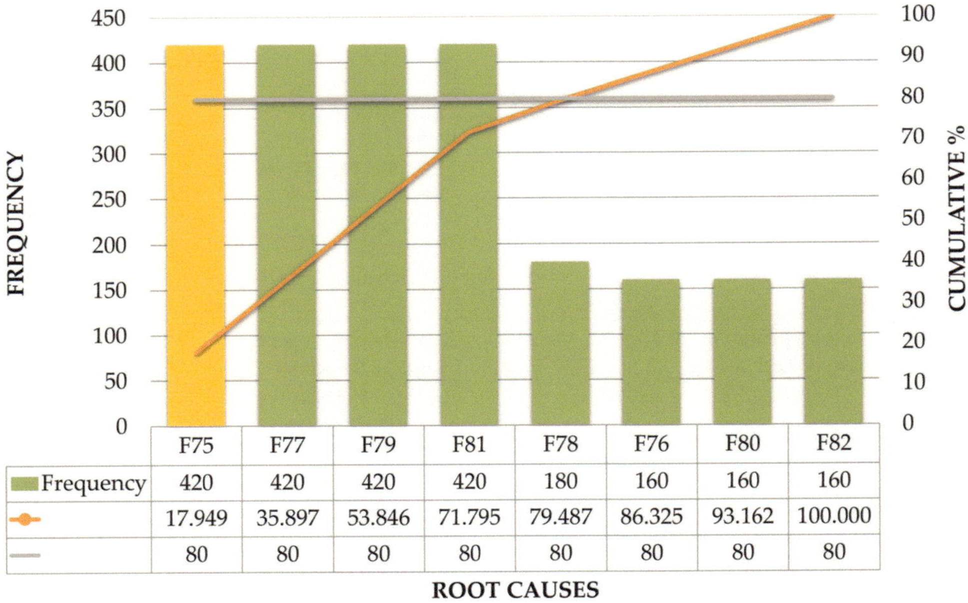

Figure 25.
Pareto analysis of initial PRN from F75 to F82.

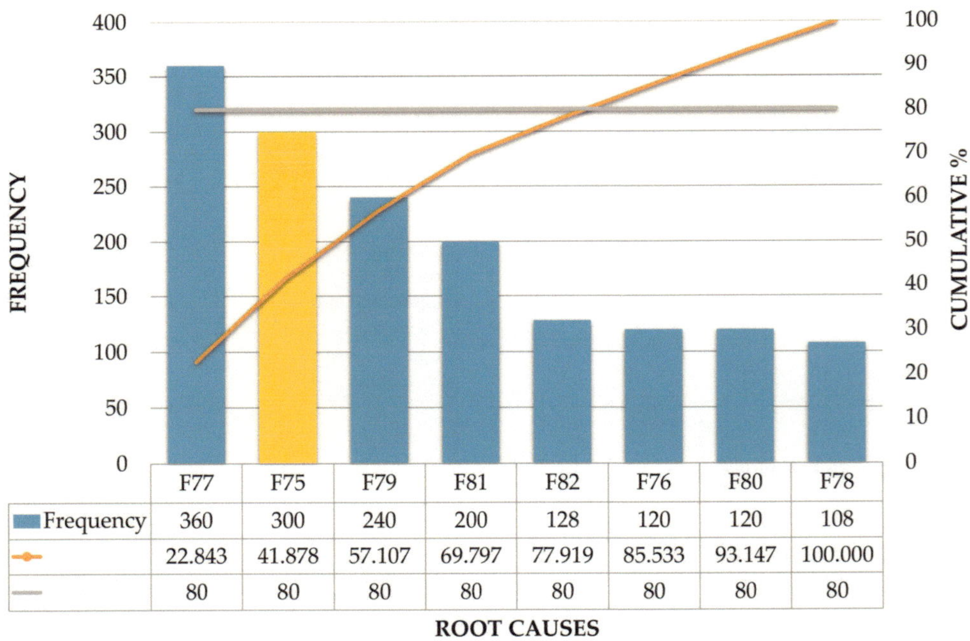

Figure 26.
Pareto analysis of residual PRN from F75 to F82.

13. Ineffective process management: emergency management

The provision of logistics services involves interrelated processes and relationships between goods suppliers, distributors, transport organisations, wholesalers, and retailers. A logistics system can only operate effectively and efficiently when all processes throughout the customer's product supply chain are functioning properly. Failure of any process in the supply chain has the potential to negatively impact the entire system and threaten the achievement of the set objectives. It is undeniable that logistics systems internationally are becoming increasingly vulnerable and open to many sources of threats. The high uncertainty in supply and demand due to the spread of the pandemic has further worsened the conditions for the smooth functioning of the supply chain and triggered the need for urgent commodity deliveries and, in some cases, threatened overall food security. Disasters, accidents, and catastrophes of various kinds create challenges for logistics systems to respond quickly and to repackage activities. **Table 11** presents the results of a risk analysis related to ineffective process management—inconsistencies and emergencies.

The experts determined the highest levels of initial PRN for factor F86, which is associated with an undefined non-conforming score. The consequences of contingency-induced risks triggered by events that are often beyond the company's control can severely compromise logistics operations and business existence. Unfortunately, managing them is not always about the logistics organisation taking measures and decisions to manage them but about taking the necessary measures at the source of the event and countermeasures in the whole economy. These negative events can occur both accidentally and as a result of permanent minor changes. Taking this into account, it is possible that, once the risk has been contained, a return

Consequences	**Initial PRN (Figure 27)**					**Actions to manage risks and opportunities**	**Residual PRN (Figure 28)**				
	No	**T**	**B**	**O**	**PRN**		**No**	**T**	**B**	**O**	**PRN**
Changes in the internal and/ or external context of the organisation (increase or decrease in scope without a plan to implement the changes)	F83	9	8	6	432	Analyse any possible implications of the changes and Improve forms of communication with clients in the contract implementation process, e.g., regular joint (service delivery) workshops	F83	7	8	6	336
Failure of the service delivery process	F84	9	8	8	576	Resource adequacy analysis and development and implementation of an ISO 45001 HSE management system	F84	7	8	8	448
Sabotage in the delivery process or loss of customer loyalty during the service delivery process	F85	8	5	9	360	Enhance staff motivation and develop and implement elements of the ISO 10002 complaints handling system	F85	6	5	9	270
Unidentified non-compliant result	F86	10	9	8	720	Improve control methods and non-compliant process of labelling production or service delivery protocol; increase staff motivation through training	F86	8	9	8	576

Table 11.
Ineffective process management: inconsistencies and emergencies.

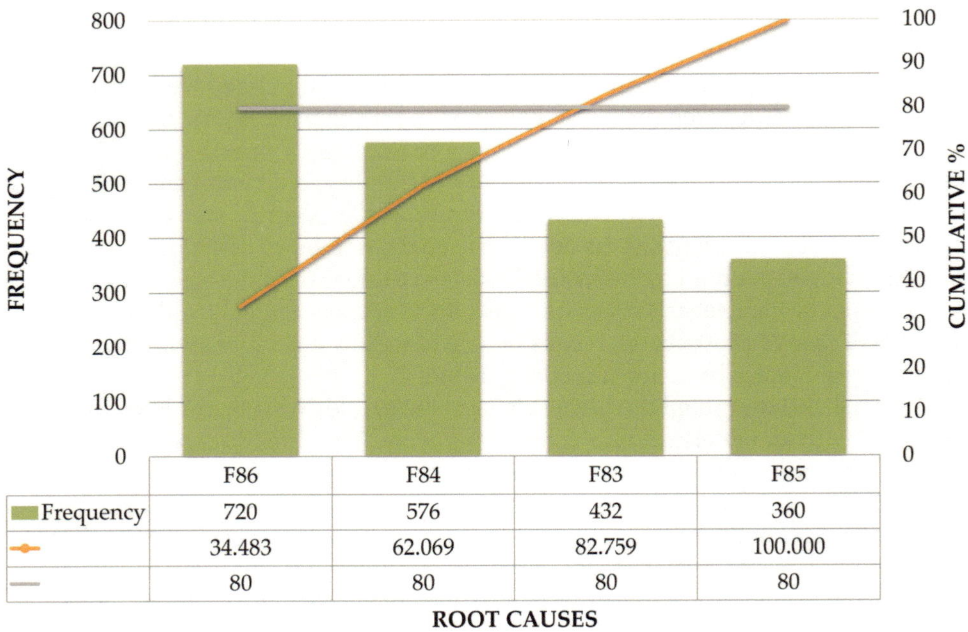

	F86	F84	F83	F85
Frequency	720	576	432	360
	34.483	62.069	82.759	100.000
	80	80	80	80

Figure 27.
Pareto analysis of initial PRN from F83 to F86.

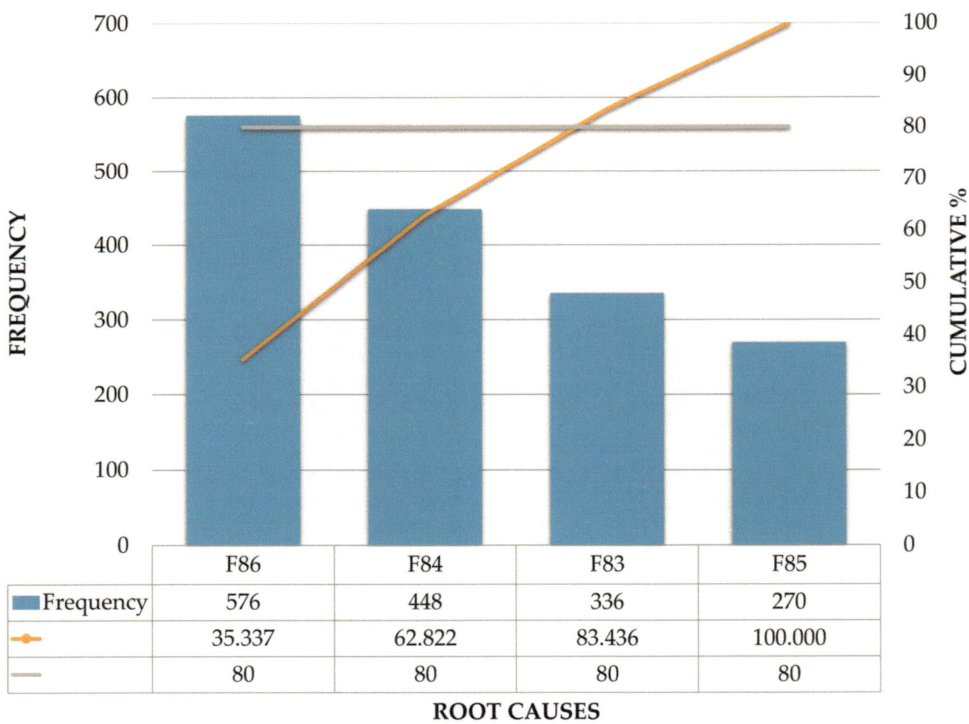

	F86	F84	F83	F85
Frequency	576	448	336	270
	35.337	62.822	83.436	100.000
	80	80	80	80

Figure 28.
Pareto analysis of residual PRN from F83 to F86.

to the original state of logistics activity may not be an adequate solution to the changed circumstances. Therefore, from the perspective of the organisation's strategic interest, it may be more appropriate not to adapt to change and rather create a new development opportunity and a completely changed logistics service delivery system.

This would be an appropriate solution in the drastically changed operating environment and conditions such that the original situation has become unfavourable, and adaptation of the system is not possible.

14. Ineffective process management: Internal audits

The ineffectiveness of internal audits of management systems in logistics is related to the fact that auditors are focused on compliance against a standard applicable to the system and documentation demonstrating such compliance, rather than on identifying opportunities for improvement. Better audit performance can be achieved when the audit programme is focused on identifying opportunities for improvement and adding value over and above the control of compliance against a standard. **Table 12** presents the results of a risk analysis related to ineffective process management: internal audits.

The highest level of initial PRN was determined by the experts for factor F88, related to the lack of qualified persons to conduct the audit. During an internal audit, unqualified auditors would find it difficult to identify and prioritise the problems and ascertain their root causes. Preventive actions against risk should be planned and implemented after an internal audit. It is good practice to re-audit the process where problems have been identified and establish the effectiveness of the corrective actions taken. In cases where the problems are not yet resolved, rather than new corrective actions, a root cause analysis by experts in the field must be conducted to avoid the consequences of identified non-conformities being compounded. Effective internal audits can help to optimise processes and, consequently, provide an effective mechanism to implement changes and improvements and contribute to increased competitiveness.

Consequences	Initial PRN (Figure 29)					Actions to manage risks and opportunities	Residual PRN (Figure 30)				
	No	T	B	O	PRN		No	T	B	O	PRN
Incorrect definition of the scope and programme of the audit	F87	7	5	3	105	Increase the competence of internal auditors and motivate internal auditors	F87	7	4	3	84
Lack of qualified persons to conduct the audit	F88	7	8	4	224	Train internal auditors. Hire auditors from external organisations	F88	5	7	2	70
Failure to state a discrepancy	F89	7	6	3	126	Increase the competence of internal auditors and motivate internal auditors	F89	6	5	3	90

Table 12.
Ineffective process management: internal audits.

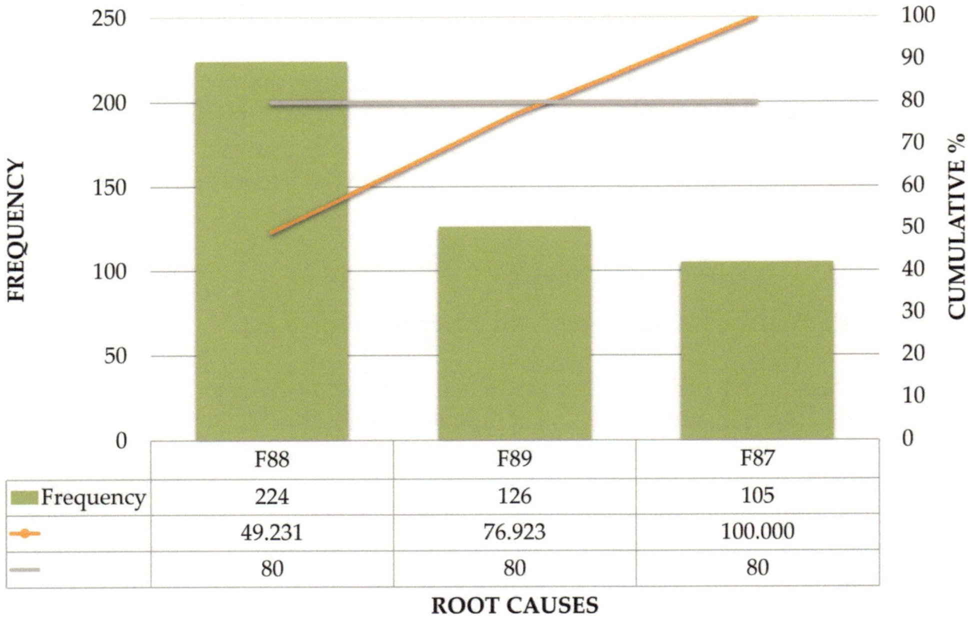

Figure 29.
Pareto analysis of initial PRN from F87 to F89.

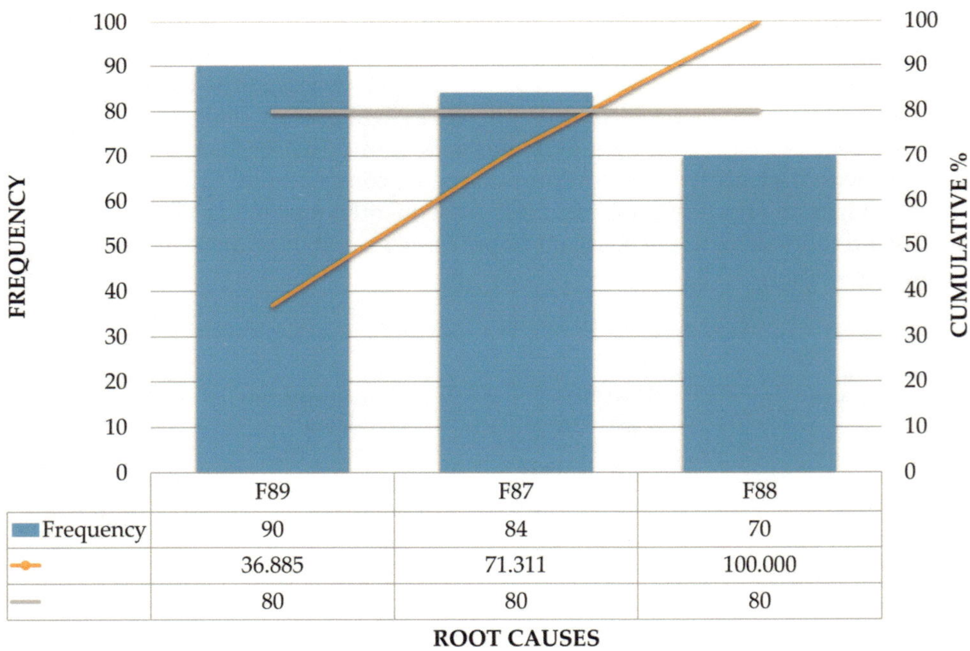

Figure 30.
Pareto analysis of residual PRN from F87 to F89.

15. Ineffective process management: leadership, management, and control

The results of the customer satisfaction survey and the opinion of experts involved in risk analysis validate the rule that to improve the quality of logistics services, it is necessary to identify and comply with customer service expectations and service performance, which positively affects customer satisfaction. Problems in management arise in cases where performance cannot meet inflated service expectations. To take action and minimise the risk of this non-conformance involves building a robust system to track orders from receipt of a request to delivery feedback such that problems and conditions that compromise satisfactory customer performance can be acted upon quickly. Management, including the control of customer-compliant logistics services, is the complete cycle of planning, executing, and controlling the efficient, cost-effective flow of raw materials, supplies, and commodities from point of origin to customer delivery and reverse logistics. The competitiveness of services can be achieved through control of the organisation's available strategic resources (including human resources) or value-creation activities [93–95]. Logistics organisations should concentrate their efforts not only on the physical delivery of the goods but on resolving any issues that arise, which are of significant concern to the customer, during delivery. Notably, different customers have different essential requirements for logistics services, which are also dynamic over time. This requires a process of continuous improvement and control of service performance. Increased control must be established in response to every case of disruption and complaint. The areas that require continuous improvement are operational efficiency and integration throughout the supply chain. **Table 13** presents the results of a risk analysis related to ineffective process management: management, service delivery process management, and strategic control.

Experts identified the highest levels of initial PRN as a factor for providing non-conforming goods or services to customer requirements. In the satisfaction analysis, this risk factor was analysed in detail. The experts, who conducted the analysis, have suggested increasing the implemented process control measures and improvements to

Consequences	**Initial PRN (Figure 31)**					**Actions to manage risks and opportunities**	**Residual PRN (Figure 32)**				
	No	**T**	**B**	**O**	**PRN**		**No**	**T**	**B**	**O**	**PRN**
Mixing mismatched and matched results	F90	9	9	9	729	Review and update the list of controlled process parameters and continuously improve the qualifications of process operators	F90	9	8	4	288
Providing non-conforming output and providing non-conforming service to customers	F91	10	10	9	900	Analysis and improvement of process control and monitoring methods and process management improvement	F91	10	10	6	600
Increased after-sales service and claims costs	F92	10	6	4	240	Process resource adequacy analysis	F92	10	6	2	120
Conflict with stakeholder interests	F93	8	6	6	288	Alignment of decisions with stakeholder interests	F93	8	6	4	192
Failure to achieve a strategic objective	F94	10	9	8	720	Optimise the frequency and depth of analysis of the organisation's decision-making context	F94	10	9	5	450

Consequences	Initial PRN (Figure 31)					Actions to manage risks and opportunities	Residual PRN (Figure 32)				
	No	T	B	O	PRN		No	T	B	O	PRN
Failure to meet quality objectives for compliance with customer requirements	F95	10	10	8	800	Improving methods for planning and analysing the adequacy of resources in processes	F95	10	10	7	700
Contraction of activity or delay in development	F96	10	9	6	540	Analysis of all possible consequences of the changes	F96	10	9	5	450
Failure to comply with the general conditions laid down in the approved contracts	F97	10	8	9	720	Resource adequacy analysis for service delivery	F97	10	8	5	400
Lack of human resources to manage and control processes	F98	9	7	8	504	Train and improve the competency of process owners and operators and optimise the frequency and depth of management review in the service delivery process	F98	9	6	4	216
Failure to comply with decisions taken	F99	10	9	8	720	Improve planning methods and optimise management review frequency	F99	10	6	6	360
Untapped market development opportunities (emerging niche markets)	F 100	10	9	9	810	Optimise management review frequency and programme to monitor changes in market conditions	F 100	10	8	8	640

Table 13.
Ineffective process management.

minimise the risk. The main area for development and sustainability is the improvement of any logistics process. Improvement processes should be linked to identified areas where non-conformities have been raised during internal audits. Certain criteria should be considered to prioritise their implementation: economic—reducing logistics costs, technological—reducing storage and transport time, organisational—improving communication and information flow, social—improving customer service, and environmental—reducing waste [96–100]. The experts involved in the study highly rate determining the residual risks for the factor related to the failure to meet quality targets for compliance with customer requirements and the risk now occupies the first position.

16. Managing common risks

Quality of service and, consequently, increasing customer satisfaction is a difficult process to standardise and depends on many factors. Non-conforming services should be avoided because they may cause a negative customer reaction that is not under the

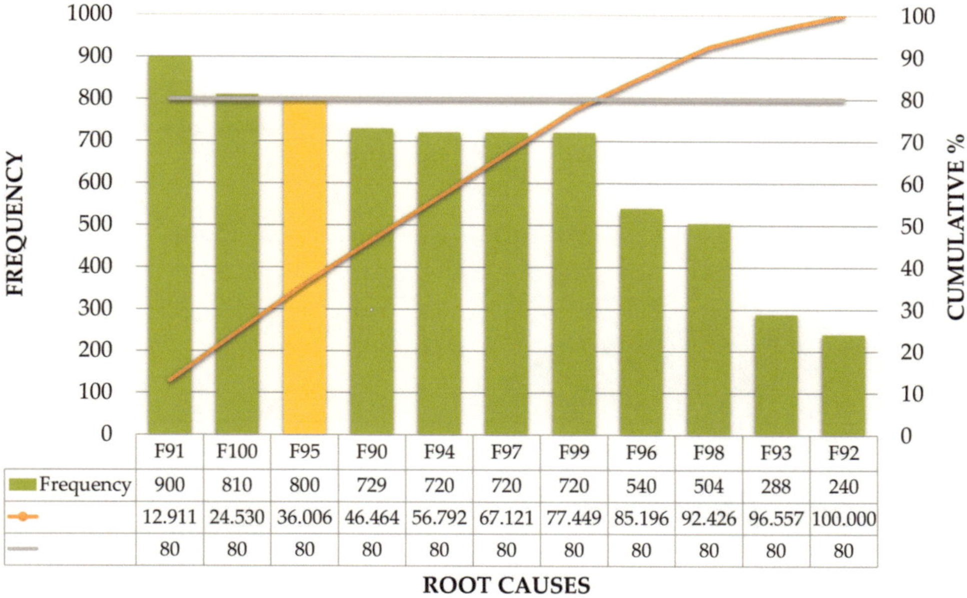

	F91	F100	F95	F90	F94	F97	F99	F96	F98	F93	F92
Frequency	900	810	800	729	720	720	720	540	504	288	240
	12.911	24.530	36.006	46.464	56.792	67.121	77.449	85.196	92.426	96.557	100.000
	80	80	80	80	80	80	80	80	80	80	80

Figure 31.
Pareto analysis of initial PRN from F90 to F 100.

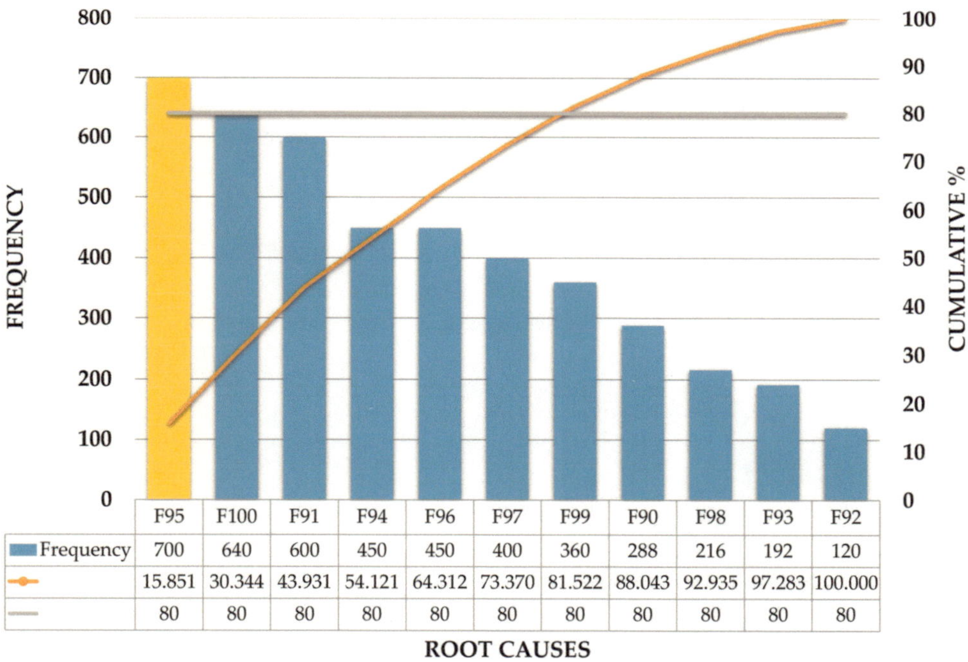

	F95	F100	F91	F94	F96	F97	F99	F90	F98	F93	F92
Frequency	700	640	600	450	450	400	360	288	216	192	120
	15.851	30.344	43.931	54.121	64.312	73.370	81.522	88.043	92.935	97.283	100.000
	80	80	80	80	80	80	80	80	80	80	80

Figure 32.
Pareto analysis of residual PRN from F90 to F 100.

control of the logistics organisation. The FMEA analysis of the risk factors that contribute to non-conformities can be used to design programmes and take actions to minimise the effects of the 100 (F01 to F100) risks investigated.

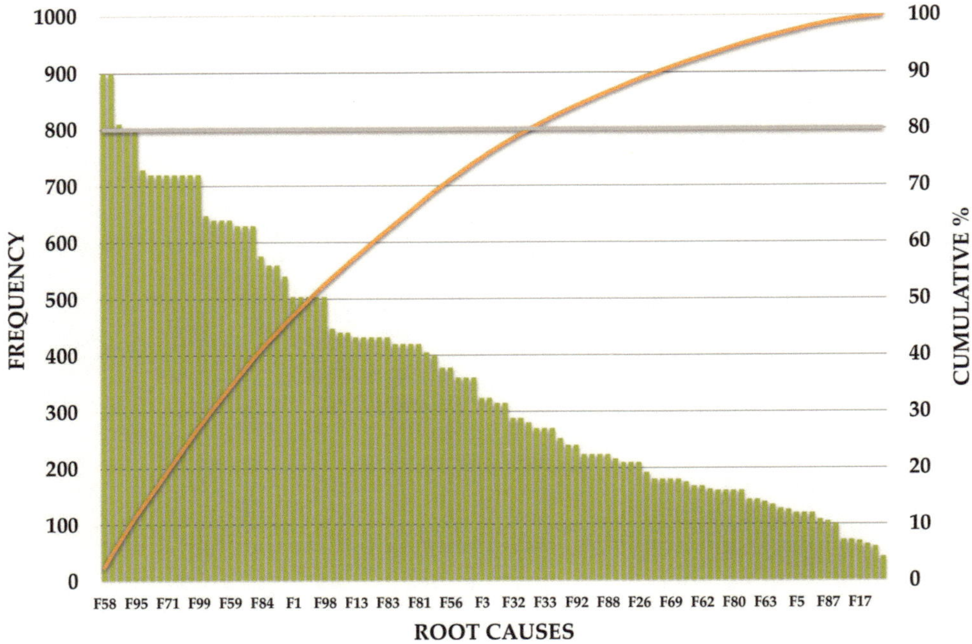

Figure 33.
Pareto analysis of initial PRN from F01 to F100.

The summary data from the initial and residual PRN analysis are presented in **Figures 33** and **34**. Results from the analysis identify the reasons that are most likely to contribute to the deterioration of the quality and satisfaction of logistics services—specifically, the occurrence of supply chain risk that is beyond the control of the

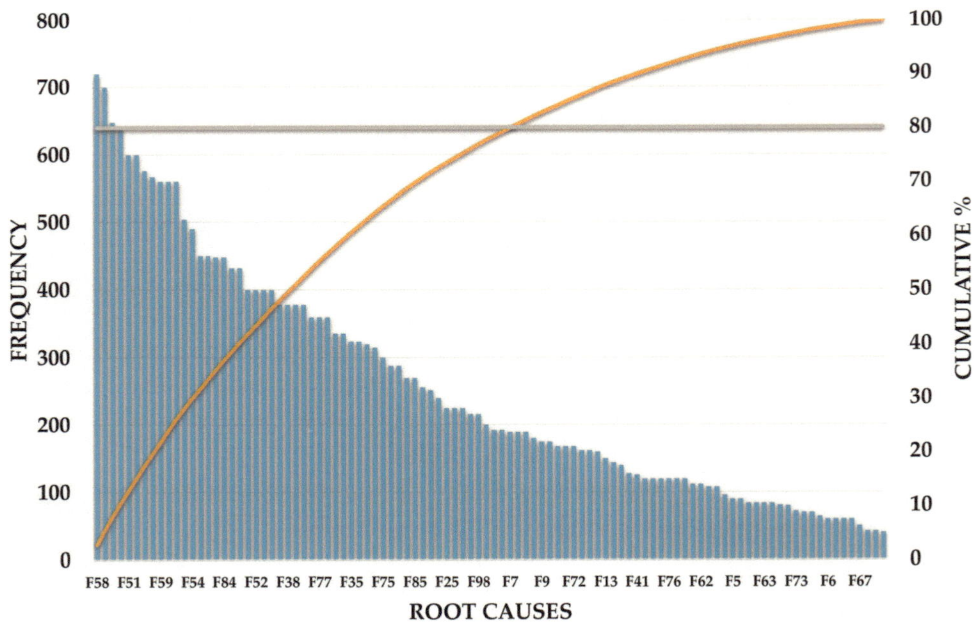

Figure 34.
Pareto analysis of residual PRN from F01 to F100.

logistics company and the provision of inadequate service to customers. All factors are analysed in more detail by main indicators.

Applying FMEA to non-conforming logistics processes and services, which have the potential to reduce satisfaction, can significantly shorten the analysis of the causes of non-conforming service quality to take timely and adequate measures before the negative impact of risk. Therefore, to improve the overall quality of logistics services through the FMEA analysis, it is necessary to identify not only the significant risks that arise from customer complaints but also specific actions to manage risks and uncover opportunities, and, subsequently, take risk management measures after corrective actions are in place.

17. Conclusion

For organisations providing logistics services, dynamic changes in the external environment impact process performance risk and threaten effective integration of resources, coordinated management of operations, and, consequently, negatively impact customer satisfaction and loyalty. These processes call for an improvement of logistics service management in the food sector and an integrated management concept combining the integration of satisfaction analysis processes and the risks that can negatively impact the delivery of a satisfying logistics service.

Due to the increasing market competition, a necessary condition for increasing customer satisfaction is the provision of qualified services that help to organise timely deliveries of the goods requested by the customer. The analyses conducted to give us reason to believe that the development of a systematic approach, including both satisfaction analysis and risk factor analysis, may be sufficient grounds for initiating improvements in customer service.

The management of improvement processes and the containment of service failure must be based on the current knowledge base and new innovative technologies. In cases where identified risks cannot be managed, a strategic development direction can be taken to outsource processes and minimise risk. Processes to improve customer satisfaction should only be undertaken after a thorough analysis to identify the root cause and determine specific actions to reduce the negative impact of potential customer service inconsistencies. Through process controls, these processes could help to prevent non-conforming services from occurring prior to customer requirements.

Logistics management has the misconception that reducing complaints would increase satisfaction to the same extent. Models for positively influencing satisfaction should contain much more than one variable. The customer satisfaction model used in this study contains six latent variables. Four observed variables are the causes of satisfaction analysis—perceived quality, value, image, and customer expectations, while the consequences of satisfaction are—complaints and loyalty. The study of customer opinion in relation to their satisfaction with logistics services and the associations between observed and latent variables are described using a set of equations with unknown coefficients. The estimated coefficient estimates were obtained using Partial Least Squares Path Modelling (PLS-PM). The calculations were performed by using XLSTAT 2021.4.1 software, which was used to determine path coefficients and the magnitude of the impact of the variables on each other and their significance.

After the analyses were performed using the SERVQUA model, the results were used for risk analysis (FMEA) to identify the causes, assessment, and consequences of logistics services that do not meet customer expectations. FMEA analysis was used as a method to investigate the consequences of emerging risks by quantifying the severity, likelihood of occurrence, and detection of non-conforming logistics services that further generated the RPN. The data from the analysis are summarised in tables by process and the results show the factors that could contribute most to potential non-conformities. Suggestions for specific actions to manage risks and opportunities that can be used for optimisation or improvement are also provided.

From the analyses, it can be concluded that the main reasons for the decline in customer satisfaction are poorly managed logistics processes caused by the lack of sufficiently competent employees ready to deal with emerging risks and human errors. Service improvement must go through an assessment and prioritisation of each element for improvement, take corrective action to manage risks, revise plans and processes in line with changes and in accordance with customer requirements, and, subsequently, examine whether the improvements have had a significant impact on satisfaction levels with the logistics services.

Acknowledgements

First, I would like to thank my family for coping with my absence during the writing of this monograph and especially my husband Daniel Stefanov, without whose support I would not have been able to realise this idea.

A huge thank you to my colleagues at the Department of Management and Logistics for encouraging this project.

I also thank all the logistics companies and users of logistics services who participated in the survey and shared their experiences.

I thank all the scientific contributors who provided constructive criticism of my work and made valuable contributions to its completion.

I also thank the "N. Vaptsarov" Naval Academy for opening opportunities and providing access to world-class educational and scientific resources and assistance from distinguished professors with scientific interests in the field of my research.

Thank you to all the organisations that hired me as a consultant and helped me strive for lifelong learning.

Conflict of interest

The author declares no conflict of interest.

Author details

Marieta Stefanova
Department "Management and Logistics", Nikola Vaptsarov Naval Academy, Varna, Bulgaria

*Address all correspondence to: m.stefanova@nvna.eu

References

[1] Mikušová M. Do small organizations have an effort to survive? Survey from small Czech organizations. Economic Research-Ekonomska Istraživanja. 2013; **26**:59-76. DOI: 10.1080/1331677X.2013. 11517630

[2] Jaques T. Chapter 14: The leadership role in crisis prevention. In: DuBrin AJ, editor. Handbook of Research on Crisis Leadership in Organizations. Cheltenham: Edward Elgar Publishing; 2013. pp. 270-310

[3] Tomasini R, Van Wassenhove L. From preparedness to partnerships: Case study research on humanitarian logistics. International Transactions in Operational Research. 2009;**16**:549-559. DOI: 10.1111/j.1475-3995.2009.00697.x

[4] Orre K. The logistics of food supply following radioactive fallout. Journal of Environmental Radioactivity. 2005;**83**: 429-432. DOI: 10.1016/j.jenvrad.2004. 05.022

[5] Dimitrakiev D, Nikolova N, Tenekedjiev K. Simulation and discrete event optimization for automated decisions for in-queue flights. International Journal of Intelligent Systems. 2010;**25**:460-487

[6] Smith M. The European Union, Crisis Management, and International OrderI. In: M Tjnar, editor. The Palgrave Handbook of EU Crises, Cham: Springer; 2021. pp. 707–723

[7] Van Wassenhove L. Humanitarian aid logistics: Supply chain management in high gear. Journal of the Operational Research Society. 2006;**57**:475-489. DOI: 10.1057/palgrave.jors.2602125

[8] Koronis E, Ponis S. Better than before: The resilient organization in crisis mode. JBS. 2018;**39**:32-42. DOI: 10.1108/JBS-10-2016-0124

[9] Boersma K, Wolbers J. Foundations of Responsive Crisis Management: Institutional Design and Information. In: Stern E, editor. Oxford Encyclopaedia of Crisis Analysis. Oxford, UK: Oxford University Press; 2021. pp. 1-25. DOI: 10.1093/acrefore/9780190228637. 013.1610

[10] Ghaderi Z, King B, Hall C. Crisis preparedness of hospitality managers: Evidence from Malaysia. Journal of Hospitality and Tourism Insights. 2021: 1-9. DOI: 10.1108/JHTI-10-2020-0199 [ahead of print]

[11] Chopra S, Sodhi M. Supply-chain breakdown. MIT Sloan Management Review. 2004;**46**:53-61

[12] Christopher M. Logistics and supply chain management. 1st-st ed. London: Financial Times/Irwin Professional Pub; 1992

[13] Pearson C, Mitroff L. From crisis prone to crisis prepared: A framework for crisis management. In: Mars DWG, editor. Risk Management. 1st ed. London: Routledge; 2019. pp. 185-196

[14] Narleva K. Entrepreneurship And Human Resourcemanagement: Approaches And Paradigms. Sustainable Human Resource Management in the Contemporary Economic Reality. 2019; **2019**:60-69

[15] Ding MJ, Kam BH, Zhang JY, Jie F. Effects of human resource management practices on logistics and supply chain competencies – evidence from China logistics service market. International Journal of Production Research. 2015;**53**:

2885-2903. DOI: 10.1080/00207543.2014.946569

[16] Nguyen H. Human resource management of logistics in Vietnam: Status and policy solutions. Human Resource Management. 2020;**11**:569-583

[17] Nilsson F. Logistics management in practice – towards theories of complex logistics. The International Journal of Logistics Management. 2006;**17**:38-54. DOI: 10.1108/09574090610663428

[18] Sellberg C, Lindmark O, Rystedt H. Training Skills and Assessing Performance in Simulator-Based Learning Environments. Switzerland: Springer Nature; 2017

[19] Arnaudova M. Diagnostic challenges in assessing post-traumatic stress disorder. Journal of IMAB–Annual Proceeding Scientific Papers. 2015;**21**: 987-990. DOI: 10.5272/jimab.2015214.987

[20] Kanev D. Social Policy and Public Choice. Germany: University Library LMU Munich; 2016

[21] Belev B, Stoyanov V. The education in "navigation" specialty at nikola vaptsarov naval academy in the terms of covid-19. Strategies for Policy in Science and Education-Strategii Na Obrazovatelnata I Nauchnata Politika. 2020:**28**(5):481-500

[22] Stoyanov V. Live through of the students in the conditions of pandemic of COVID – 19. Strategies for Policy in Science and Education-Strategii Na Obrazovatelnata I Nauchnata Politika. 2021;**29**:154-171. DOI: 10.53656/str2021-2-3-pan

[23] Mednikarov B. Current trends in the maritime profession and their implications for the maritime education. Proceedings of the International Association of Maritime Universities Conference. 2019;**1**:275-286

[24] Kanev D. Seaborne trade effects of international terrorism and effectiveness of the anti-terrorist policy. Accident Analysis & Prevention. 2005;**40**:594-601

[25] Stoyanov V. Coping with stress at different levels of work stress. Journal VFU. 2011:1-15

[26] Kanev D. External Stimuli and Internal Motivation. Economy and Economic Theory: Problems and Interactions, Conference Proceedings. 2017;**1**:47-57

[27] McAfee R, Glassman M, Honeycutt J. The effects of culture and human resource management policies on supply chain management strategy. Journal of Business Logistics. 2002;**23**:1-18. DOI: 10.1002/j.2158-1592.2002.tb00013.x

[28] Kilibarda M, Pajić V, Andrejić M. The influence of online shopping determinants on customer satisfaction in the Serbian market. International Journal for Traffic and Transport Engineering. Human Resources in Logistics and Supply Chains: Current State and Trends. 2019;**9**:270-279

[29] Anastasiou S. Critical human resources management functions for efficient logistics and supply chain management. Katerini, Greece: Proceedings of the 2nd International Conference on Supply Chains; 2012

[30] Kampf R, Ližbetinová L. The identification and development of talents in the environment of logistics companies. NAŠE MORE: Znanstveni Časopis Za More i Pomorstvo. 2015;**62**: 139-142

[31] Stoyanov V. Psihichen stres v organizatsiyata. 1st ed. VSU

Chernorizets Hrabar: Varna, Bulgaria; 2011

[32] Kmytiuk T, Inna S, Bilyk T. An integrated approach to logistic risk assessment. Economic Journal of Lesya Ukrainka Volyn National University. 2021;**1**:161-174

[33] Tenekedjiev K, Nikolova N, Dimitrakiev D. Theory and Practice of Risk Decisions. Varna, Bulgaria: Mars Soft and Publishing; 2002

[34] Breuer C, Siestrup G, Haasis H, Wildebrand H. Collaborative risk management in sensitive logistics nodes. Team Performance Management. 2013; **19**:331-351. DOI: 10.1108/TPM-11-2012-0036

[35] Bartosova T, Taraba P, Peterek K. Approach to the risk management process in logistics companies. Chemical Engineering Transactions. 2021;**86**: 403-408

[36] Bolgova E, Haitbaev V, Nikishchenkov S. Big data analytics in the model "Cargo flow—transport and logistics infrastructure." In: Mantulenko SIAV, editor. Current AchievementsChallenges and Digital Chances of Knowledge Based Economy. Cham: Springer; 2021. pp. 405-413

[37] Pereira V, Narayanamurthy G, Ishizaka A, Yassine N. Decision Making in Logistics Management in the Era of Disruptive Technologies. The International Journal of Logistics Management. 2021;**32**:305-319. DOI: 10.1108/IJLM-05-2021-487

[38] Kohli R. Block-3 Logistics Management: Emerging Trends. In: Medury PU, editor. Logistics Management. New Delhi: Indira Gandhi National Open University, School of Social Sciences; 2021. pp. 124-173

[39] Ballard RL. Methods of inventory monitoring and measurement. Logistics Information Mngt. 1996;**9**:11-18. DOI: 10.1108/09576059610116653

[40] Lutz S, Löedding H, Wiendahl H. Logistics-oriented inventory analysis. International Journal of Production Economics. 2003;**85**:217-231. DOI: 10.1016/S0925-5273(03)00111-7

[41] Defee C, Williams B, Randall WS, Thomas R. An inventory of theory in logistics and SCM research. Int Jrnl Logistics Management. 2010;**21**:404-489. DOI: 10.1108/09574091011089817

[42] Abrahamsson M, Aronsson H. Measuring Logistics Structure. International Journal of Logistics Research and Applications. 1999;**2**: 263-284. DOI: 10.1080/1367556990 8901585

[43] Caplice C, Sheffi Y. A review and evaluation of logistics performance measurement systems. Int Jrnl Logistics Management. 1995;**6**:61-74. DOI: 10.1108/09574099510805279

[44] Dimitrakiev D, Stankov V, Atanasova C. Procedures for improving safety in the shipping activities. SCNVNA. 2017;**32**:5-11

[45] Weng J. Exploration of Innovative development of logistics management in the internet age. In: Kacprzyk J, editor. International Conference on Applications and Techniques in Cyber Security and Intelligence. Cham: Springer; 2021. pp. 173-179

[46] Ayantoyinbo B, Gbadegesin A. Examination of the effect of logistics functions on financial performance of organization. Int J Eng Tech Mgmt Res. 2021;**8**:18-26. DOI: 10.29121/ijetmr.v8.i3.2021.875

[47] Istiqomah S, Viana AB, Cahyati AN, Susanti SD. Application Scorecard Logistics Method for Comparative Analysis of Performance Measurement: A Case Study. Singapore: IEOM Society International; 2021

[48] Ailawadi SC, SINGH PR. Logistics and Supply Chain Management. Phagwara, New Delhi: PHI Learning Pvt. Ltd.; 2021

[49] McKinnon AC. The Influence of Logistics Management on Freight Transport Research A Short History of a Paradigm Shift. Journal of Transport Economics and Policy. 2021;**55**:104-123

[50] Song DP. Container Logistics and Maritime Transport. 1st ed. London: Routledge; 2021

[51] Dimitrakiev D, Atanasova K. Planning aspects of maritime of maritime transport activities. Industrial Management. Technical University of Sofia. 2015;**12**:78-84

[52] Wantanakomol S. The effect of guidelines on reducing logistics costs. Uncertain Supply Chain Management. 2021;**9**:667-674. DOI: 10.5267/j.uscm.2021.5.003

[53] Nonaka I. A dynamic theory of organizational knowledge creation. Organization Science. 1994;**5**:14-37. DOI: 10.1287/orsc.5.1.14

[54] Manhart M, Thalmann S. Protecting organizational knowledge: A structured literature review. Journal of Knowledge Management. 2015;**19**:190-211. DOI: 10.1108/JKM-05-2014-0198

[55] Kanev D. The Paradox Of Information. Vol. 14. "Neofit Rilski." Blagoevgrad: Economics and Management, Faculty of Economics, South-West University; 2018. pp. 59-73

[56] Mednikarov B, Tsonev Y, Lazarov A, Lazarov A. Analysis of Cybersecurity Issues in the Maritime Industry. Information & Security: An International Journal. 2020;**47**:27-43. DOI: 20200924053840237

[57] Jagodzińska N. Implementing information security management systems in transport industry organizations. Transport Economics and Logistics. 2020; **82**:79-90. DOI: 10.26881/etil.2019.82.07

[58] Prokopowicz D, Gołębiowska A, Matosek M. Growing importance of digitization of remote communication processes and the internetization of economic processes and the impact of the SARS-CoV-2 (Covid-19) coronavirus pandemic on the economy. Warszawa: Publishing House SGSP; 2021. pp. 221-250

[59] Daugherty PJ, Ellinger AE, Gustin CM. Integrated logistics: Achieving logistics performance improvements. Supp Chain Mnagmnt. 1996;**1**:25-33. DOI: 10.1108/13598549610155297

[60] Kent JL. Leverage 2: interfunctional co-ordination between logistics and information technology. Int Jnl Phys Dist & Log Manage. 1996;**26**:63-78. DOI: 10.1108/09600039610128276

[61] Okoh P. Infrastructure Asset Management. Integrated logistics support and asset management (ILSAM) 2019;**6**(4):245-257

[62] Daugherty P, Myers M, Richey R. Information support for reverse logistics: The influence of relationship commitment. Journal of Business Logistics. 2002;**23**:85-106. DOI: 10.1002/j.2158-1592.2002.tb00017.x

[63] Turker D, Altuntas C. Sustainable supply chain management in the fast

fashion industry: An analysis of corporate reports. European Management Journal. 2014;**32**:837-849. DOI: 10.1016/j.emj.2014.02.001

[64] Ellinger AE, Daugherty PJ, Gustin CM. The relationship between integrated logistics and customer service. Transportation Research Part E: Logistics and Transportation Review. 1997;**33**: 129-138. DOI: 10.1016/S1366-5545(97) 00012-4

[65] Ahi P, Searcy C. A comparative literature analysis of definitions for green and sustainable supply chain management. Journal of Cleaner Production. 2013;**52**:329-341. DOI: 10.1016/j.jclepro.2013.02.018

[66] Awaysheh A, Klassen RD. The impact of supply chain structure on the use of supplier socially responsible practices. Int Jrnl of Op & Prod Mnagemnt. 2010;**30**:1246-1268. DOI: 10.1108/01443571011094253

[67] Dubey R, Gunasekaran A, Papadopoulos T, Childe SJ, Shibin KT, Wamba SF. Sustainable supply chain management: Framework and further research directions. Journal of Cleaner Production. 2017;**142**:1119-1130. DOI: 10.1016/j.jclepro.2016.03.117

[68] Rajeev A, Pati R, Padhi S, Govindan K. Evolution of sustainability in supply chain management: A literature review. Journal of Cleaner Production. 2017;**162**:299-314. DOI: 10.1016/j.jclepro.2017.05.026

[69] Choy K. Managing uncertainty in logistics service supply chain. International Journal of Risk Assessment and Management. 2007;**7**:19-43. DOI: 10.1504/IJRAM.2007.011408

[70] Tijan E, Aksentijević S, Ivanić K, Jardas M. Blockchain technology implementation in logistics. Sustainability. 2019;**11**:1185-1194. DOI: 10.3390/su11041185

[71] Jugović TP, Hadžić AP, Ogrizović D. Importance and effects of the electronic documents implementation in the service of logistics-forwarder operator. Pomorstvo. 2009;**1**:221-242

[72] Dziea G, Sikora M, Nowak A. The Implementation of the Enterprise Resource Planning System and its Influence on Logistics. Studies & Proceedings of Polish Association for Knowledge Management, Bydgoszcz. 2016;**82**:38-48

[73] Mednikarov B, Dimitrov N, Vasilev V. Security analysis of the national maritime transportation system as part of maritime critical infrastructure. Barcelona: 119-Th Annual General Assembly of the International Association of Maritime Universities IAMU; 2018. pp. 343-351

[74] Gimenez C, Ventura E. Logistics-production, logistics-marketing and external integration: Their impact on performance. International Journal of Operations & Production Management. 2005;**25**:20-38. DOI: 10.1108/ 01443570510572222

[75] Flynn BB, Huo B, Zhao X. The impact of supply chain integration on performance: A contingency and configuration approach. Journal of Operations Management. 2010;**28**:58-71. DOI: 10.1016/j.jom.2009.06.001

[76] Stoyanova A, Kirechev D. Contemporary challenges for the sustainable production and supply of wooden pallets in Bulgaria. Bingley, West Yorkshire, England: Emerald Group Publishing Limited; 2020

[77] Selviaridis K, Spring M. Third party logistics: A literature review and research agenda. The International Journal of Logistics Management. 2007; **18**:125-150. DOI: 10.1108/09574090710748207

[78] Selviaridis K, Spring M. Supply chain alignment as process: Contracting, learning and pay-for-performance. International Journal of Operations & Production Management. 2018;**38**:732-755. DOI: 10.1108/IJOPM-01-2017-0059

[79] Evan WM. Non-Contractual Relations in Business: A Preliminary Study. American Sociological Review. 1963;**28**:67. DOI: 10.2307/2090459

[80] Andersson D, Norrman A. Procurement of logistics services—a minutes work or a multi-year project? European Journal of Purchasing & Supply Management. 2002;**8**:3-14. DOI: 10.1016/S0969-7012(01)00018-1

[81] Boysen S, Corsi T, Dresner M, Rabinovich E. Managing effective third party logistical relationships: What does it take? Journal of Business Logistics. 1999;**20**:73-101

[82] Jüttner U, Peck H, Christopher M. Supply chain risk management: Outlining an agenda for future research. International Journal of Logistics Research and Applications. 2003;**6**: 197-210. DOI: 10.1080/13675560310001627016

[83] Ogorelc A, Logožar K. Outsourcing of logistics activities in manufacturing industry. Promet-Traffic & Transportation. 2001;**13**:387-394

[84] Abdur Razzaque M, Chen SC. Outsourcing of logistics functions: A literature survey. Int Jnl Phys Dist & Log Manage. 1998;**28**:89-107. DOI: 10.1108/09600039810221667

[85] Jaafar HS, Rafiq M. Logistics outsourcing practices in the UK: A survey. International Journal of Logistics Research and Applications. 2005;**8**: 299-312. DOI: 10.1080/13675560500407283

[86] Rabinovich E, Windle R, Dresner M, Corsi T. Outsourcing of integrated logistics functions: An examination of industry practices. International Journal of Physical Distribution & Logistics Management. 1999;**29**:353-374. DOI: 10.1108/09600039910283587

[87] Kirechev D. Agri-environmental practices for land use as a prerequisite for building a sustainable agri-food system. Trakia Journal of Sciences. 2021;**19**: 207-215

[88] van Damme DA, Ploos van Amstel MJ. Outsourcing logistics management activities. The International Journal of Logistics Management. 1996;**7**:85-94. DOI: 10.1108/09574099610805548

[89] Jawab F, Arif J. Risk matrix model applied to the outsourcing of logistics' activities. JIEM. 2015;**8**:1179-1194. DOI: 10.3926/jiem.1485

[90] de Boer L, Gaytan J, Arroyo P. A satisficing model of outsourcing. Supp Chain Mnagmnt. 2006;**11**: 444-455. DOI: 10.1108/13598540610682462

[91] Mello J, Stank T, Esper T. A model of logistics outsourcing strategy. Transportation Journal. 2008;**47**:5-25

[92] Cho J, Ozment J, Sink H. Logistics capability, logistics outsourcing and firm performance in an E-commerce market. International Journal of Physical Distribution & Logistics Management. 2008;**38**:336-359. DOI: 10.1108/09600030810882825

[93] Stoilov D. Process Approach-Prevention or Response. In: Quality Management of Plant Protection Activities. Varna, Bulgaria: University Publishing House; 2021

[94] Pauliková A. Innovative Approaches to Model Visualization for Integrated Management Systems. Sustainability. 2021;**13**:8812

[95] Zafirova T. Strategic decisions in the crisis stages of the organization. Izvestia Journal of the Union of Scientists - Varna Economic Sciences Series. 2020;**9**: 100-108. DOI: 10.36997/IJUSV-ESS/2020.9.1.100

[96] Prokopowicz D, Gołębiowska A. Increase in the Internetization of economic processes, economic, pandemic and climate crisis as well as cybersecurity as key challenges and philosophical paradigms for the development of the 21st century civilization. Journal of Modern Science. 2021;**47**(2):307–344

[97] Marinova V, Stoyanova A. Paper recycling in Covid-19 conditions. Izvestia Journal of the Union of Scientists-Varna Economic Sciences Series. 2020;**9**:43-52

[98] Marinova V, Stoyanova A, Radev R, Zhivkova V. Quality of goods and digital consumption-prospects and disadvantages. Economic Science, Education and the Real Economy: Development and Interactions in the Digital Age. 2020;**1**:693-706

[99] Kirechev D. Impact of climate change on the development of the agrarian sector–adaptation and mitigation measures. Izvestia Journal of the Union of Scientists-Varna Economic Sciences Series. 2017;**1**:111-125

[100] Golebiowska A, Jakubczak W, Prokopowicz D, Jakubczak R. The post-pandemic development of the green circular economy and the declarations made during the UN climate change conference (COP26) as security determinants. European Research Studies Journal. 2021;**XXIV**:251-275. DOI: 10.35808/ersj/2655